Best Easy Day Hikes
Fairbanks

Help Us Keep This Guide Up to Date

Every effort has been made by the author and editors to make this guide as accurate and useful as possible. However, many things can change after a guide is published—trails are rerouted, regulations change, facilities come under new management, etc.

We would love to hear from you concerning your experiences with this guide and how you feel it could be improved and kept up to date. While we may not be able to respond to all comments and suggestions, we'll take them to heart and we'll also make certain to share them with the author. Please send your comments and suggestions to the following address:

The Globe Pequot Press
Reader Response/Editorial Department
P.O. Box 480
Guilford, CT 06437

Or you may e-mail us at:

editorial@GlobePequot.com

Thanks for your input, and happy trails!

Best Easy Day Hikes Series

Best Easy Day Hikes
Fairbanks

Montana Hodges

FALCONGUIDES ®

GUILFORD, CONNECTICUT
HELENA, MONTANA
AN IMPRINT OF THE GLOBE PEQUOT PRESS

FALCONGUIDES ®

Copyright © 2009 by Morris Book Publishing, LLC

Falcon, FalconGuides, and Outfit Your Mind are registered trademarks of Morris Book Publishing, LLC.

Maps created by Designmaps Inc. © Morris Book Publishing, LLC

Library of Congress Cataloging-in-Publication Data is available on file.

ISBN: 978-0-7627-5105-1

Printed in the United States of America

10 9 8 7 6 5 4 3 2 1

Contents

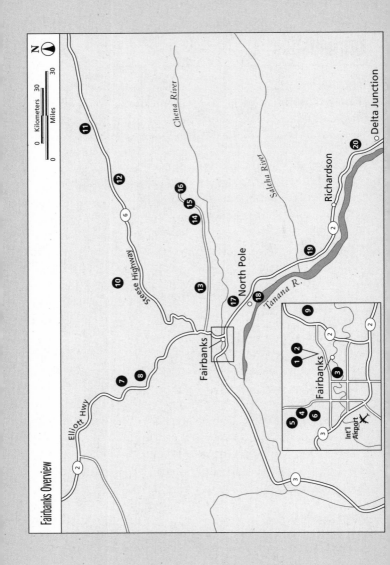

Fairbanks Overview

N

0   Kilometers   30
0   Miles   30

Elliott Hwy

Steese Highway

Chena River

Salcha River

Tanana R.

Fairbanks

North Pole

Richardson

Delta Junction

Int'l Airport

Introduction

This book contains twenty hikes all within two hours of Fairbanks, ranging from thirty-minute strolls to day-long adventures. There is an abundance of hiking opportunities in this immense region, from city trails aside dancing sandhill cranes to high climbs into the tundra. To the north of the city the great White Mountains National Recreation Area beckons hikers with a million acres, and hundreds of trail miles. The Chena River State Recreation Area covers over 400 square miles of pristine public stomping ground and is home to some of the region's most popular easy day hikes. At the cusp of this state land, the private Chena Hot Springs Resort operates a free system of nearly a dozen trails open to the public and is home to the steaming hot mineral pools that have been soothing the aching limbs of hikers for generations.

Nestled within the sprawling Tanana Valley, just a dip below the Arctic Circle, Fairbanks is Alaska's most centrally located metropolis and the largest city in the interior. For this reason, Fairbanks has been unofficially sloganed the "Hub of the Interior." Fairbanks centers not just the land, or the recreational delights; it centers the people and communities of the interior. This leads to Fairbanks's official name "The Golden Heart City." Combining friendly outdoor-oriented people, a dry climate, and nearly never-ending summer daylight, Fairbanks truly is Alaska's Golden Heart.

Weather and Sunlight

To hike in Fairbanks, not only do you need to understand weather in the interior, but also the amount of daylight you may experience. Fairbanks is a short 130 miles from the Arctic Circle. During peak summer hiking months, the sun can linger above the horizon over twenty-one hours a day. During this time, it does not get completely dark for the few hours the sun dips below the horizon and you will find twenty-four hours a day of usable light.

Fairbanks is in a dry subarctic climate zone. Mid- to late summer are always the friendliest times to hike, and on some trails the only time to hike without snow. It is not uncommon, especially at high elevations, for the snow to remain on the trail through spring, and then begin falling again in August. For this reason, it is always important to check with land managers before heading out to remote areas. Consistently summer is the warmest and most popular time to hike. Most wildflowers are blooming in early to mid-summer. Late summer and fall can also be spectacular. The fall colors and infamous fireweed blooms of these northern latitudes are hard to beat, not to mention the unsurpassed berry picking. Many people, non-hikers included, will trek to the farthest edge of some trails in mid- to late August filling buckets with berries. Fall can be chilly, but the color displays and delicious berries are hard to beat, even if the sun is setting by 10:00 p.m.!

Wilderness Restrictions/Regulations

There are dozens of popular hikes in the Fairbanks area. Of these, only a handful are well labeled with trailheads. In Fairbanks you won't find any national parks or monuments. Many trails are on Bureau of Land Management or Department of Natural Resources land. These managers operate a more loosely maintained system of trails than their cousins at federal and state parks. Always be sure to contact the land managers in advance to check the status of the trails. Never rely on these trails being well labeled. Bring maps, a GPS, a compass, and a sense of adventure.

Alaska State Parks also operates a substantial chunk of the area's hiking trails. You'll find these routes more polished and developed; they are also more regulated, and there is generally a fee. The Fairbanks North Star Borough operates similarly well-maintained routes with small day use fees.

Safety and Preparation

Maps

Rough maps are included in this book. These maps are meant to serve as an overview of hiking locations. You will need to purchase more specific ones for each area you visit. You can purchase maps from the Geophysical Institute Map Office/Earth Science Information Center on the University of Alaska–Fairbanks campus in the International Arctic Research Center at 930 Koyukuk Drive, (907) 474-6960. Along with these maps be sure to bring a GPS and a compass.

Wildlife

Bears, caribou, moose, and wolves, along with small mammals and hundreds of species of birds, are all possible to see from Fairbanks area trails. Fairbanks is home to both black and brown bears. Many of these bears are acclimated to human interaction and bear attacks are rare; fatal bear attacks are especially rare.

Bears are curious creatures; they are attracted to odors, especially of food. To avoid bears eliminate odors as much as possible. Bears also don't like surprises. Exercise caution and common sense. Most encounters can be avoided with the proper precautions. Always make your presence known, and never put yourself in a position where you could surprise a bear. Make lots of noise. Use your voice, probably the most effective bear repellent there is.

People often seem comfortable walking within a few yards of a moose to snap a photo, but this is extremely dangerous. Moose, especially cows with calves, are known to charge. These big-legged stampeders can be fatal. Never approach a moose. If you come across one on a trail give way to the beast and change your course.

Fairbanks is close to the Arctic, and mosquitoes in the northern latitudes are notorious. Prepare for bugs from spring through late fall. Never leave without your bug spray and a soothing bite gel. If you'll be trekking into the least bit of swampy territory, consider bringing a head net.

Clothing

Whatever season you hike in Fairbanks, layering is the way to go. Layering prepares you for all sorts of weather and keeps things lightweight. Synthetic fibers are a must. Wet cotton does not insulate. For the base layer choose a long-sleeved synthetic shirt and pants designed to wick away moisture from your body. On top of this you can add an insulating layer, fleece, and a warm vest. The outer layer should be a waterproof shell. If weather is chilly you can always add thermals under the base along with gloves and a hat. Bring both a warm waterproof hat and sun hat. Don't forget sunblock and lip balm for the interior's long summer days.

Secure, comfortable and well-fitted footwear is essential for hiking. Wandering around the wilderness with exposed toes or inadequate shoes could cause any number of accidents. Depending on your activity and your choice of trail, you may want hiking boots or running shoes or something in between. For whatever your level requires, make sure that your shoes are waterproof, or prepare for wet feet. The risk of wet feet leads to one of the most important items—socks. Wool socks are best because they still insulate even if they get wet. Again, if not wool, stick with synthetics and avoid cotton.

Survival Gear

Bring the essential survival gear on your hikes outside the city. Carry a day pack with water and extra clothing. A good trail pack includes a water purifier, compass, emergency blanket, pocket knife, waterproof matches, first-aid kit, and safety whistle. The weather shifts quickly in the interior, and even on established routes it is not uncommon for hikers to become lost or disoriented. Be prepared for anything.

Zero Impact

Probably the most valuable thing for hikers and nature is observing the "Zero Impact" backcountry ethic. Exercise these principles and you'll get along fine on any trail in Alaska. The following is a simplified version of Falcon's zero-impact principles pertaining to hiking in Fairbanks.

Leave with Everything You Brought

Never leave any material behind, no matter how small or biodegradable the item. Whether it is a gum wrapper or an apple core, these sights sorely degrade the quality of the hike for others and disturb Mother Nature. Bring sealed containers and bags for packing out all your waste; garbage receptacles are not always available. Always pick up after pets. Oftentimes, negligent pet owners force land managers to omit pet-friendly trails. Every trail in this book allows dogs—this is an honor and great responsibility.

Leave No Sign of Your Visit
Park only in designated areas and use only designated facilities. Always stay on the trail; if the trail is muddy or wet, walk through it anyway. Stepping off the trail damages the surrounding vegetation and widens your impact. Never cut switchbacks; cutting switchbacks offsets erosion control.

Leave the Landscape as You Found It
Collecting materials of any kind can be illegal along some trails. Always check the regulations before you pick berries. Don't pick flowers or peel birch bark. Leave the trail beautiful and natural for the next user.

How to Use This Guide

This guide is designed to be simple and easy to use. Each hike is described with a map and summary information that delivers the trail's vital statistics including distance, difficulty, fees and permits, schedule, canine compatibility, and trail contacts. Directions to the trailhead are also provided, along with a general description of what you'll see along the way. A detailed route finder (Miles and Directions) sets forth mileages between significant landmarks along the trail.

Difficulty Ratings

These are all easy hikes, but easy is a relative term. To aid in the selection of a hike that suits particular needs and abilities, each is rated easy, moderate, or more challenging. Bear in mind that even the most challenging hike can be made easy by hiking within your limits and taking rests when you need them.

- **Easy** hikes are generally short and flat, taking about an hour to complete.
- **Moderate** hikes involve increased distance and relatively small changes in elevation, and will take one to two hours to complete.
- **More challenging** hikes feature some steep stretches and generally take longer than two hours to complete.

These are completely subjective ratings—keep in mind that what you think is easy is entirely dependent on your level of fitness and the adequacy of your gear (primarily shoes). If you are hiking with a group, you should select a hike with a rating that's appropriate for the least fit and prepared in your party.

Approximate hiking times are based on the assumption that on flat ground, most walkers average 2 miles per hour. Adjust that rate by the steepness of the terrain and your level of fitness (subtract time if you're in good shape and add time if you're hiking with kids), and you have a ballpark hiking duration. Be sure to add more time if you plan to picnic or take part in other activities like bird watching or photography.

Trail Finder

Best Hikes for Children

Best Hikes for Dogs

Best Hikes for Geology Lovers

Best Hikes for Hot Springs

Best Hikes for Great Views

Best Hikes for Nature Lovers

Map Legend

===②===	State Highway
	Local/Forest Roads
= = = =	Unimproved Road
- - - - - -	Trail
■-■-■-■	Featured Route
——	River/Creek
⬭	Lake/Pond Fill
	Marsh/Swamp
▭	County and State Forest/Park
⚓	Boat Launch
⏝	Bridge
▲	Campground
●–●	Gate
❷	Information Center
⛴	Observation Towers
℗	Parking
▲	Peak/Rock Formation
⊼	Picnic Area
■	Point of Interest/Other Trailhead
⑂	Restrooms
❻	Trailhead
⬿	Viewpoint
N ⬆	True North (Magnetic North is approximately 15.5° East)

1 Farm Road Trail and Chickadee Loop

The Creamer's Field Migratory Waterfowl Refuge offers the best birding in the Fairbanks region along a small system of easy urban trails. Each year over 150 different species of birds at some point call this farm home, a third of which can be seen in the short summer season. Sandhill cranes and Canada geese have trademarked the refuge and flock here in the hundreds from spring through fall. The level and easy Farm Road Trail cuts incredibly close to these brilliant birds: Don't forget the camera!

Distance: 2.3-mile lollipop
Approximate hiking time: 1 to 2 hours
Difficulty: Easy
Trail surface: Gravel, dirt
Best season: Spring through fall
Other trail users: Runners
Canine compatibility: Leashed dogs permitted
Fees and permits: No fees or permits required
Schedule: Open year-round, but some portions of the refuge are closed to hikers during fall and spring bird migration. In winter some trails are groomed for skiers, mushers, and skijoring.

Maps: USGS Fairbanks D-2, Alaska Department of Fish and Game's brochure Creamer's Field Guide to Summer, or Alaska Bird Observatory's interpretive guide Chickadee Loop Trail
Trail contacts: Alaska Department of Fish and Game, 1300 College Road, Fairbanks, AK 99701; (907) 459-7213; www .adfg.state.ak.us; Friends of Creamer's Field, Farmhouse Visitor Center, 1300 College Road, Fairbanks, AK 99701; (907) 452-5162; www.creamersfield .org

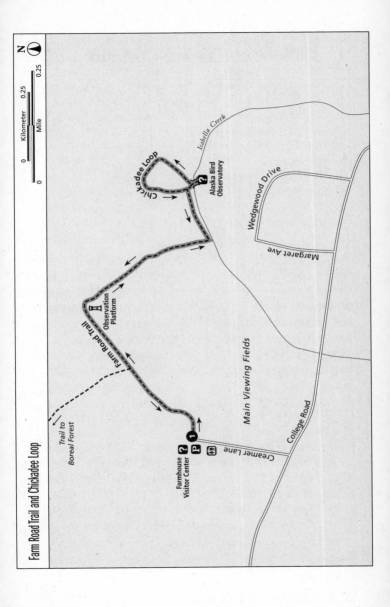

Farm Road Trail and Chickadee Loop

Finding the trailhead: Creamer's Field is on College Road not far from the Steese Highway. Depending on where you are in the city there are many ways to reach it. From the Steese Highway/Expressway (Highway 2) at mile 1 take College Road west 1.6 miles and turn right onto the short access road into Creamer's Field and the dead-end at the Farmhouse Visitor Center. The main trailhead is to the right of the parking area at GPS coordinates N64 51.817' / W147 44.252'. You can pick up your maps and guides at the visitor center ($1 donation).

The Hike

Birders rejoice! Fairbanks has a treat for you—the Creamer's Field Migratory Waterfowl Refuge. The turn-of-the-twentieth-century farm was once the largest dairy in the interior. Over time the farm attracted a substantial population of migratory birds including thousands of cranes, geese, and ducks who utilize the seeded fields and wetlands as feeding and staging grounds each year. When the dairy was up for sale in the 1960s, the Alaska Department of Fish and Game took over the property to develop a refuge, much to the community's applause. The refuge now encompasses 1,800 acres and is home to the Alaska Bird Observatory. The original farmhouse has been transformed into a visitor center and the property is on the Fairbanks National Register of Historic Places.

When the Canada geese roll into town it is front page news, and for many in Fairbanks, the definitive sign of spring. From spring through fall, ducks, geese, swans, and cranes, along with dozens of other species of birds, take their break here between feeding grounds. Not far from the city center, the birding of Creamer's Field is something of a local hotspot and it is a landmark place to hike within town.

This hike begins at the main trailhead across the parking lot from the Farmhouse Visitor Center; be sure to stop and pick up the interpretive guide. The Farm Road Trail almost immediately cuts through the open grain fields, often thick with cranes and geese. The giant birds may swoop overhead, or be within footsteps of hikers. Be sure to give way to these wild animals, and keep your pets leashed, calm, and controlled at all times.

Around the half-mile mark is a story-high viewing platform perched over the fields. This is a nice place to stop and take in the big picture or quietly enjoy nature's music. Below, the trail stretches past another grain field before its conclusion at the edge of a spruce forest. To the right a bridge leads to the Alaska Bird Observatory and the Chickadee Loop is to the left. For a cool crisp spurt in the forest add on the 0.3-mile Chickadee Loop. The soft woodchip trail hosts an easy walk through a towering forest home to . . . you guessed it, numerous boreal chickadees! Their distinctive song will certainly be heard. There is also an option to park at the Alaska Bird Observatory and hike only the Chickadee Loop.

Miles and Directions

0.0 Begin at main trailhead near the Farmhouse Visitor Center and restroom. Head northeast on the Farm Road Trail, staying right at the Y.

0.3 Footpath to left is a shortcut to Boreal Forest Loop. Stay right.

0.6 Story-high wildlife observation deck.

0.8 Follow the trail left as it corners.

1.0 End Farm Road Trail at intersection with Chickadee Loop. Alaska Bird Observatory/ Chickadee Loop trailhead is to right across footbridge over Isabella Creek. Begin Chickadee Loop.

1.3 End Chickadee Loop, and follow the Farm Road Trail right.

2.3 Arrive back at the main trailhead.

2 Boreal Forest and Seasonal Wetland Trail

Creamer's Field Migratory Waterfowl Refuge offers numerous trails. This second selection is a combination of two easy hikes showcasing contrasting ecosystems. The Boreal Forest Trail travels along boardwalks and dirt paths through the thick boreal forest. The more exposed Seasonal Wetland Trail travels past the largest wetlands on the property. Both easy trails have wheelchair accessible options.

Distance: 2.9-mile lollipop and out-and-back combo (with shorter and longer options)
Approximate hiking time: 2 hours
Difficulty: Easy
Trail surface: Dirt, boardwalk
Best season: Spring through fall
Other trail users: Runners
Canine compatibility: Leashed dogs permitted
Fees and permits: No fees or permits required
Schedule: Open year-round, but some portions of the refuge are closed to hikers during fall and spring bird migration. In winter some trails are groomed for ski-ers, mushers, and skijoring.
Maps: TOPO! Alaska CD 5, USGS Fairbanks D-2, Friends of Creamer's Field's brochure Creamer's Field Guide to Summer, and interpretive guide The Boreal Forest Trail
Trail contacts: Alaska Department of Fish and Game, 1300 College Road, Fairbanks, AK 99701; (907) 459-7213; www .adfg.state.ak.us; Friends of Creamer's Field, Farmhouse Visitor Center, 1300 College Road, Fairbanks, AK 99701; (907) 452-5162; www.creamersfield .org

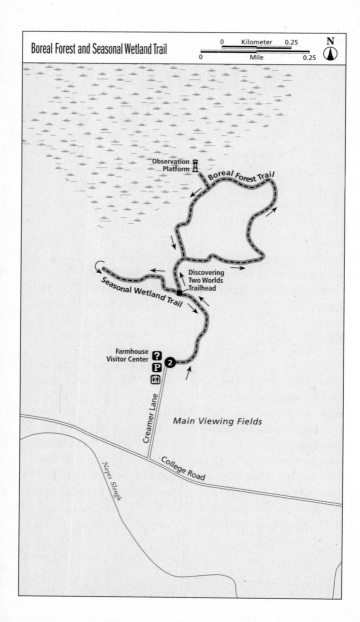

Finding the trailhead: Creamer's Field is on College Road not far from the Steese Highway. Depending on where you are in the city there are several ways to reach it. From the Steese Highway/ Expressway (Highway 2) at mile 1 take College Road west 1.6 miles and turn right onto the short access road into Creamer's Field and the dead-end at the Farmhouse Visitor Center. The main trailhead is to the right of the parking area at GPS coordinates N64 51.817' / W147 44.252'. You can pick up your maps and guides at the visitor center ($1 donation).

The Hike

The "Discovering Two Worlds" combination encases two premier hikes at Creamer's Field Migratory Waterfowl Refuge. The trails spawn from the same trailhead but travel through dueling ecosystems and an array of habitats.

The Boreal Forest Trail easily treks through a portion of the world's most extensive forest. An extremely informative twenty-two-page interpretive guide follows corresponding numbers along this trail. On the hike look for all six species of interior trees along with dozens of wildflowers. Depending on the time of year, the boardwalks may balance over the flooded forest floor; at other times the flourishing willows are the only reminder of the moist habitat. Wildlife viewing might be best in spring, but during midsummer this is a superbly shady break from the stretching hours of sun.

The more exposed Seasonal Wetland Trail leads across the Western Viewing Fields beside a vernal pond toward the Alaska Bird Observatory Bird Banding Station. Here you'll find iris and early summer wild "prickly" rose, tall grasses, and a chance to see more shorebirds and waterfowl. The scenery will change dramatically throughout the year. Wetlands along the field bustle with life in spring.

To reach these routes begin at the main trailhead across the parking lot from the Farmhouse Visitor Center. Take the trail north from the parking lot that cuts through the Main Viewing Fields, where sandhill cranes and Canada geese congregate. Have your Boreal Interpretive Trail guide in hand; the numbers begin as soon as you enter the field. A nearly immediate Y links to the Farm Road Trail to the right; stay left for the Discovering Two Worlds Trail. The trailhead is on your right 0.3 mile in.

Miles and Directions

0.0 From the main trailhead enter the field and stay left at the Y with the Farm Road Trail; interpretive numbers begin here.

0.3 Discovering Two Worlds trailhead. Go right for Boreal Forest Trail loop, left for Seasonal Wetland out-and-back.

1.8 Return from Boreal Forest Trail, go right for Seasonal Wetland.

2.2 End Seasonal Wetland.

2.6 Return to Two Worlds trailhead.

2.9 Arrive back at the main trailhead.

3 Chena River Bike Trail

This bike path pumps through the golden heart of Fairbanks showcasing downtown's main attractions and the lovely Chena River. The portion described stretches from Pioneer Park through Golden Heart Plaza past the World War II memorial to the cusp of Fort Wainwright. The route is level, paved, and popular year-round for recreation and commuting.

Distance: 7.0 miles out and back (with shorter options)
Approximate hiking time: 3 hours
Difficulty: Easy
Trail surface: Paved
Best season: Spring through fall
Other trail users: Runners, cyclists
Canine compatibility: Leashed dogs permitted
Fees and permits: No fees or permits required
Schedule: Open year-round
Maps: TOPO! Alaska CD 5, Alaska Department of Transportation's BIKEWAYS: Fairbanks, North Pole and Vicinity (available at the Log Cabin Visitor Center)
Trail contacts: City of Fairbanks, 800 Cushman Street, Fairbanks, AK 99701; (907) 459-6715; www.ci.fairbanks.ak.us; Alaska Department of Transportation and Public Facilities, Northern Region Office, 2301 Peger Road, Fairbanks, AK 99709; (907) 451-2380; www.dot.state.ak.us
Special considerations: Prepare for snow October through May.

Finding the trailhead: You can hop on this trail anywhere between Pioneer Park and Fort Wainwright. If you're traveling by vehicle it is best to begin at Pioneer Park, located at the corner of Airport Way and Peger Avenue, where you can park for free. You'll find Pioneer Park roughly centered between the Parks Highway, Mitchell Expressway, and Steese Expressway. From Airport Way near the Rich-

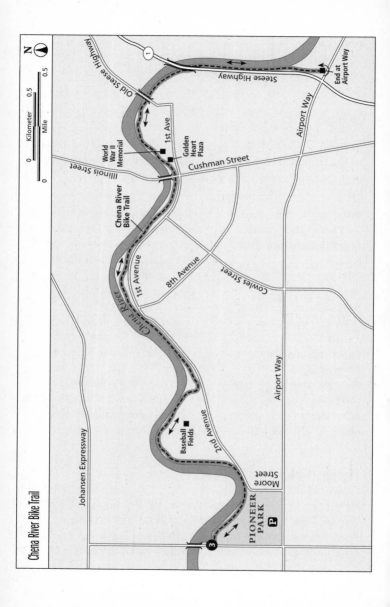

Chena River Bike Trail

ardson Highway, head west 2 miles to Pioneer Park at the corner of Peger Road. To reach the trail walk north through the property until you reach the trail along the Chena River at GPS coordinates N64 50.474' / W147 46.691'. Follow the bike path east.

The Hike

From park to park this urban trail offers the absolute best of downtown Fairbanks. Begin at Pioneer Park—formerly Alaskaland, the free theme park of Alaskan history. Here you can taste the local flavor, view art, book a show, fill up the water bottle, and take advantage of the public restrooms.

The trail is located at the northern edge of Pioneer Park. Begin along a wide paved path in a parklike setting following the Chena River channel. Aside the trail among the wild willow and alder thickets, you'll find benches, patches of groomed grass, and occasional landscaped edges. About a mile down the river the path diverts from the water just before the dog park (there are future plans to relocate this canine hotspot). From this point the trail will continue to move east along the sidewalks of 2nd Avenue through an industrial, and less scenic, clip of town. There are some interpretive signs and a couple of benches to break up the street scene. By the time you reach Golden Heart Plaza a mile farther however, the trail is in the heart of downtown and passes some lovely portions of the river.

Golden Heart Plaza is the foremost destination in downtown Fairbanks. On warm summer days the plaza makes a good stop, with dozens of relaxing benches around a striking fountain. The small plaza is dedicated to Alaska's statehood and centers many events; it is also home to the Log Cabin Visitor Center and is the hub of souvenir shops. The parklike setting of the trail continues to the World War II memorial just after the plaza. From there the route becomes more functional, serving primarily commuters. It also is increasingly more urban, with graffiti-ridden tunnels and little aesthetics.

You can readily hop on and off this easy walkway at any point in the city. The most attractive sections stretch from Pioneer Park to the dog park and from Golden Heart Plaza to the World War II memorial. These highlights can be combined into an easy 5.0-mile round-trip journey. Of course if you park at Pioneer Park remember to tack on a half mile to the round-trip to compensate for the quarter-mile walk from the trail to the car.

Miles and Directions

0.0 Begin at Pioneer Park. Head north through the park to its edge along the Chena River, and follow the bike path east.

1.2 Intersection with 2nd Avenue; after dog park, go left and follow trail along side road.

2.1 Wildlife viewing deck along river.

2.3 Intersection with Cushman Street; carefully cross Cushman Street toward the visitor center.

2.4 Reach Golden Heart Plaza.

2.5 Reach World War II memorial.

2.8 Pass under bridge.

3.0 Pass under bridge.

3.5 End at Airport Way; entrance to Fort Wainwright to left.

7.0 Arrive back at the trailhead.

4 Ballaine Lake

The spectacularly natural and wooded University of Alaska–Fairbanks campus is home to dozens of interconnecting trails with a mosaic of combinations. Ballaine Lake is a small but well appreciated lake popular with both canines and humans. An easy 1.2-mile loop through rolling hills and airy birch groves begins at the lake trailhead and travels along some of the classic winter ski routes—which are grassy and dry during the summer.

Distance: 1.2-mile loop (with shorter and longer options)
Approximate hiking time: 45 minutes
Difficulty: Easy
Trail surface: Grass, dirt
Best season: Best summer through fall
Other trail users: Runners, cyclists, horses
Canine compatibility: Leashed dogs permitted
Fees and permits: No fees or permits required
Schedule: Closed to hikers and dogs from first snow until snow melt, during which the trails are groomed for skiers. For winter-friendly hiking and dog trails see the University of Alaska–Fairbanks brochure North Campus Winter Trails.
Maps: TOPO! Alaska CD 5, USGS Fairbanks D-2, University of Alaska–Fairbanks brochure North Campus Summer Trails
Trail contacts: University of Alaska North Campus Facilities Services, 803 Alumni Drive, Fairbanks, AK 99775; (907) 474-7000; University Trails Club, P.O. Box 756640, Fairbanks, AK 99775; (907) 474-6027; www.uaf.edu/trails

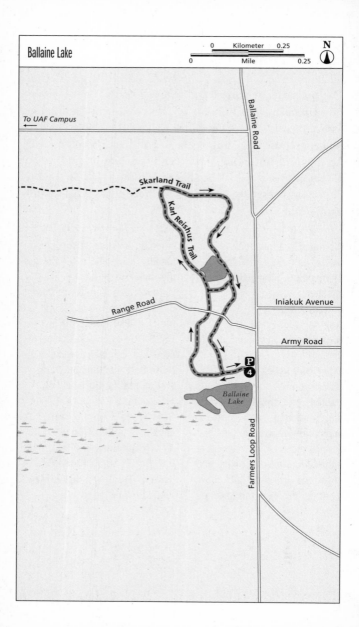

Ballaine Lake

0 — Kilometer — 0.25
0 — Mile — 0.25

N

To UAF Campus

Ballaine Road

Skarland Trail

Kari Reishus Trail

Range Road

Iniakuk Avenue

Army Road

P
4

Ballaine Lake

Farmers Loop Road

Finding the trailhead: Ballaine Lake is located on the east side of the UAF campus, along Farmers Loop Road. To reach the trailhead, from the Parks Highway/Robert Mitchell Expressway at mile 359 in central Fairbanks head north onto University Avenue. Follow University Avenue 3 miles as it becomes Farmers Loop Road. The Ballaine Lake trailhead is on your left, just before Farmers Loop and Ballaine Road merge. The trailhead is located at GPS coordinates N64 50.199' / W147 49.495'.

The Hike

Conveniently nestled in the city, on the edge of the "college" district, the 1,100-acre University of Alaska–Fairbanks campus offers escape in the heart of town. The complex trail system was pioneered by enthusiastic campus skiers in the early 1900s. In the warmer months popular romps are frequented by trail runners, horseback riders, mountain bikers, college commuters, photographers, and afternoon walkers. The web of trails is a local gem, but if you're not local it is easy to make a wrong turn and end up lost. Only a few hikes are fully labeled, and there are just a few maps throughout the miles of trails. Use the hikes described in this guide as a base to explore campus recreation, but be sure to pick up a map (or two!) before you head out.

Ballaine Lake is frequented during the peak summer months by anglers and day-hikers. The property was originally set aside for research by the geophysical institute, but today is largely a recreation area crisscrossed by trails. This loop near the lake combines pieces of the Skarland 6-mile and Karl Reishus winter ski trails, which are maintained in the summer. Both trails commemorate great campus skiers. By the 1930s UAF student Ivar Skarland had developed most of the trails in this corner, but it wasn't until he returned to teach and eventually passed away that this trail was named after him. Similarly Karl Reishus was also an enthusiastic student skier, and son of a ski coach, whose life was lost tragically at a young age. Both are memorialized on these trails, which during the winter months host serious skiers.

Begin this trail by heading west on a singletrack dirt path into a stunted spruce grove. After a couple hundred feet the path quickly meets the Karl Reishus Trail and heads north. From there the route slowly rises and falls through gentle hills in a tall white spruce and birch forest. In a little over half a mile the trail dead-ends and the Skarland 6-mile is picked up to the right. This little piece of the Skarland 6-mile passes through a small meadow of waist-high grasses. Wildflowers, mushrooms, berries, and birds all make a living in this forest; keep an eye peeled and a naturalist guide ready. On the return the road may not be seen, but the sound of cars zooming down Farmers Loop is a reminder that this forest treasure is in the city limits.

Miles and Directions

- **0.0** Begin at the Ballaine Lake parking area. Head west along the small footpath and stay left as you meet the loop trail in 200 feet, and the immediate small social trail to the lakeshore.
- **0.3** Cross over Range Road and shortly thereafter pass a singletrack trail to right. You can take this trail for an early bailout and cut the trail length in half.
- **0.6** End of Karl Reishus Trail; go right onto Skarland 6-mile.
- **1.0** Pass over Range Road.
- **1.1** Intersection with trail to trailhead/parking area to left.
- **1.2** Arrive back at the trailhead.

5 Powerline Trail

The Powerline Trail follows the highlights of hiking at the University of Alaska–Fairbanks. The 1.7-mile trail slopes away from the university's Large Animal Research Station through a spruce forest into the grassy meadows at the heart of the campus. Intersecting trails connect side-trips to the Exotic Tree Plantation, Potato Field, and Smith Lake Wildlife Preserve.

Distance: 3.2 miles out and back (with longer options)
Approximate hiking time: 2 hours
Difficulty: Easy
Trail surface: Woodchip, gravel, dirt
Best season: Summer through fall
Other trail users: Runners, cyclists, horses
Canine compatibility: Leashed pets permitted in snow-free months
Fees and permits: No fees or permits required
Schedule: Closed to hikers and dogs from first snow until snowmelt, when the trails are groomed for skiers. For winter-friendly hiking and dog trails see the University of Alaska–Fairbanks brochure North Campus Winter Trails.
Maps: TOPO! Alaska CD 5, USGS Fairbanks D-2, University of Alaska–Fairbanks leaflet North Campus Summer Trails
Contacts: University of Alaska North Campus Facilities Services, 803 Alumni Drive, Fairbanks, AK 99775; (907) 474-7000; University Trails Club, P.O. Box 756640, Fairbanks, AK 99775; (907) 474-6027; www.uaf.edu/trails

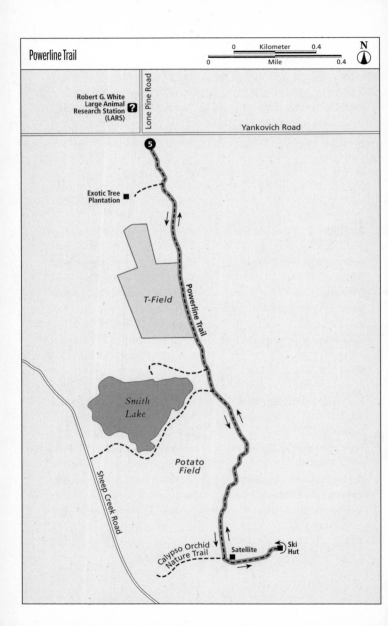

Powerline Trail

0   Kilometer   0.4

0   Mile   0.4

N

Lone Pine Road

Robert G. White
Large Animal
Research Station
(LARS) ?

Yankovich Road

5

Exotic Tree
Plantation ■

T-Field

Powerline Trail

Smith
Lake

Potato
Field

Sheep Creek Road

Calypso Orchid
Nature Trail

Satellite ■

Ski
Hut ■

Finding the trailhead: The Powerline Trail leads from the Robert G. White Large Animal Research Station (LARS) on Yankovich Road, where parking is available, to the Ski Hut at the center of campus. Depending on where you are in the city, there are many ways to reach the station. From the Parks Highway/Robert Mitchell Expressway in central Fairbanks, exit north onto University Avenue at mile 359. Follow University Avenue 3.6 miles, as it becomes Farmers Loop Road, and turn left onto Ballaine Road. Drive 0.2 mile down Ballaine Road and turn left onto Yankovich Road. Look for LARS on your right after 1 mile. Park and carefully cross the road to the trailhead, located at GPS coordinates N64 52.669' / W 147 51.931'.

The Hike

You'll find this hike across Yankovich Road from the university's Robert G. White Large Animal Research Station (LARS). The Arctic Institute of Biology, students, and scientists study many large arctic creatures including reindeer, moose, and musk oxen at the station. For a few dollars, a short tour is worth the time.

The trail heads south on a brief woodchip path, through a thick dark spruce forest. After about 125 feet the Skarland Ski Trail signs point right; stay left for the Powerline Trail, then right at the Y intersection. Just before 0.2 mile you reach the power lines and the unlabeled Powerline Trail. Although you are no longer at LARS as you trek down the hill, much of the land you cross is a living UAF research project. As the Powerline route begins, the slim trail that immediately cuts off to the right is an optional excursion leading to the Exotic Tree Plantation. The plantation dates back to the early 1960s when the Institute of Northern Forestry, a relative of the United States Forest Service, conducted a study on the productivity of exotic trees in the subarctic. Today the plantation is not maintained, but is still utilized by scientists and recreational hikers alike.

The Powerline Trail then passes through the open grassy T-Field Meadow. Named for the T shape of the field, the area was originally planted in Finnish oats. Today the beautiful meadow has a wide trail neatly mowed around the edges that is popular with trail runners. A small trail map is mounted at the far end of the T-Field. As you wander away from the map the Smith Lake Wildlife Preserve is the next attraction. At 0.8 mile a short trail to the right leads to the calm lake where you might see various species of waterfowl. You'll often notice these water-bound birds overhead on the Powerline Trail as they make their way to and from the small preserve.

The link to the Potato Field is located a mile down the trail. This field dates back to 1908 and is one of the oldest features along the Powerline Trail. Through time Potato Field has served many different niches from housing yaks, to test patches of berries to, well, potatoes—though you won't find any spuds growing there today.

You may choose to end your hike when the trail reaches the satellite at 1.4 miles. A quick turn left will take you an additional uneventful 0.2 mile to the Ski Hut where the trail officially ceases. There is also the Calypso Orchid Nature Trail to the right if you'd like to extend your day hike.

Miles and Directions

- **0.0** Begin at trailhead across from LARS.
- **0.2** Intersection with power lines.
- **0.4** Reach T-Field.
- **0.6** End T-Field, trail map to left; follow trail left onto T-Field Road.

0.8 Smith Lake to right.

1.1 Trail to right leads to Potato Field.

1.4 Reach satellite, Calypso Orchid Nature Trail access to right, Ski Hut and Powerline Trail end to left.

1.6 End at Ski Hut.

3.2 Arrive back at the trailhead.

6 Calypso Orchid Nature Trail

A botany lover's delight, this easy loop trail is located on the campus of University of Alaska–Fairbanks on a knoll above the extensive Georgeson Botanical Garden. The Calypso Orchid Nature Trail is known for a spectacular spring orchid bloom, when the rare and delicate flowers shoot from the mossy forest floor. Allow plenty of time to read the interpretive signs at any time of year.

Distance: 0.7-mile lollipop (with longer options)
Approximate hiking time: 30 minutes to 1 hour
Difficulty: Easy
Trail surface: Dirt
Best season: Summer through fall
Other trail users: Runners, cyclists, horses
Canine compatibility: Leashed dogs permitted
Fees and permits: No fees or permits required
Schedule: Closed to hikers and dogs from first snow until snow melt, when the trails are groomed for skiers. For winter-friendly hiking and dog trails see the University of Alaska–Fairbanks brochure North Campus Winter Trails.
Maps: TOPO! Alaska CD 5, USGS Fairbanks D-2, University of Alaska–Fairbanks brochure North Campus Summer Trails
Trail contacts: University of Alaska North Campus Facilities Services, 803 Alumni Drive, Fairbanks, AK 99775; (907) 474-7000; University Trails Club, P.O. Box 756640, Fairbanks, AK 99775; (907) 474-6027; www .uaf.edu/trails

Finding the trailhead: The Calypso Orchid Nature Trail is located on the west end of the University of Alaska–Fairbanks. Pick up the trail at the overlook parking area on Tanana Loop Road near the intersection of Yukon Drive. Depending on where you are in the city,

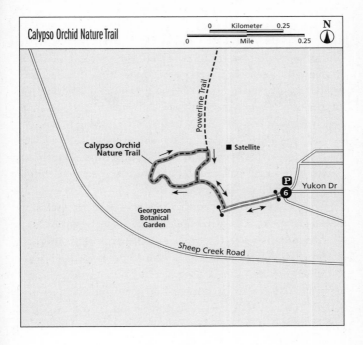

Calypso Orchid Nature Trail

Powerline Trail

Calypso Orchid Nature Trail

■ Satellite

Georgeson Botanical Garden

Sheep Creek Road

Yukon Dr

N

0   Kilometer   0.25
0   Mile   0.25

there are many ways to reach the campus. From the Parks Highway/ Robert Mitchell Expressway, exit east onto the Geist Road/Chena Pump Road at mile 356.8. Follow Geist Road 0.7 mile and turn left onto Thompson Drive. After 0.5 mile make a left onto West Tanana Loop Road/Kantishna Drive at the roundabout. Drive 0.3 mile to the overlook parking/trailhead on your left at the bend in the road, at GPS coordinates N64 51.473' / W147 51.290'.

The Hike

If you've been wondering what all those beautiful flowers, shrubs, and towering trees are in the Fairbanks region, spend an afternoon in this area of the UAF campus where the well-labeled Calypso Orchid Nature Trail offers a crash course in plant identification. From the common to the obscure, the lingonberry and Siberian peas to the quaking aspen and great white spruce, you'll find an abundance of information. Soon you will be a trail-side expert, able to point out kinnikinnik! For a real treat incorporate a walk around the Georgeson Botanical Garden, located just below the Calypso trail. A walkway easily covers the manicured garden in less than half a mile and passes by specimens ranging from giant cabbage to exotic rose.

The Calypso Orchid Nature Trail is accessed by heading west from the overlook, passing behind a gate and traveling a few hundred feet to the official trailhead through another gate on the right. The orchids bloom between mid-May and mid-June. If you have a chance to see the delicate beauties it's a site not to be missed, but if you miss the spring delight, this easy trail is good all season long. The warm sun-soaked hillside offers a dry and breezy stroll through a classic boreal forest scene. Unlike the manicured and planted garden below, the Calypso Orchid Trail follows the naturally occurring vegetation, largely labeled with small placards by Dr. Pat Holloway, who landmarked the trail in 1994. After about a half mile the interpretive signs begin to fade and cut off completely upon return. The route is labeled for the most part (a real treat in the UAF tangle of trails). Follow the circular silver markers, but don't rely on their presence; always take a map.

Miles and Directions

0.0 Head west from the parking area behind gate.

0.1 Go right through another gate to official trailhead.

0.2 Intersection with loop, go left.

0.3 Y in trail, stay right.

0.4 Junction with lighted ski trail (Big Whizzy Loop), restricted trails, and a gate to the satellite/Powerline Trail. Go right to stay on Calypso Orchid Nature Trail, following the interpretive signs.

0.5 At intersection follow trail left to trailhead.

0.6 Return to trailhead.

0.7 Arrive back at the parking area.

7 Grapefruit Rocks

This heart-pumping but immediately rewarding hike leads to spectacular vistas of the Globe Creek valley and a series of rock outcroppings popular with area rock climbers. The strenuous but short mile-long loop is heavily traveled through the summer and maintained solely by climbers.

Distance: 1.0-mile loop
Approximate hiking time: 1 hour
Difficulty: More challenging
Trail surface: Rock, dirt
Best season: Summer
Other trail users: None
Canine compatibility: Leashed dogs permitted
Fees and permits: No fees or permits required
Schedule: None
Maps: TOPO! Alaska CD 5, USGS Livengood B-3
Trail contacts: Alaska Depart-

ment of Natural Resources, Fairbanks Area Office, 3700 Airport Way, Fairbanks, AK 99709; (907) 451-2601; www.dnr.state.ak.us

Special considerations: With a couple of steep drops along the rugged trail, Grapefruit Rocks is not suitable for small children or anyone not confident with steep grades. This trail is not officially maintained and status could change at any time. There are no facilities at this trailhead.

Finding the trailhead: From Fairbanks take the Steese Highway 11 miles north to the junction with the Elliott Highway in Fox. Continue north on the Elliott Highway for 39 miles. At milepost 39 turn right onto an easy-to-miss unlabeled road at the break in the guardrails. A few hundred feet leads to the trailhead at GPS coordinates N65 17.386' / W147 10.178'.

The Hike

Grapefruit Rocks is an unofficial little loop on Alaska

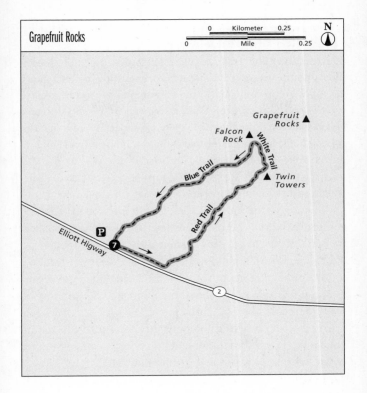

Department of Natural Resources (DNR) land. The single track trail leads to a series of rock outcroppings, known locally as "Upper Grapefruit Rocks" (lower is down the road). The route is labeled and maintained better than most official hikes—a phenomenon that attests to the popularity of these trails for climbing ascents. Recreational climbers are responsible for the development and maintenance of this trail, so the status could change at any time. In 2008 the trail was well labeled and included a trailhead showcasing the routes.

For a best easy day hike, Grapefruit Rocks should be considered on the strenuous side. The elevation rises about 500 feet over the first quarter mile. Since the trail is very short and the views are immediately rewarding, this is a good day hike if you don't mind the tough grade. The somewhat rough footing transitions from a soil to a rocky and decomposed rock trail as the grade grows steeper. Watch out for roots, rocks, and other obstacles in the bumpy track. Rock pillars poke out of the partially shaded forest, but for the most part this trail is exposed, so bring sunblock and a rain jacket, not to mention secure footwear for the climb.

There are three routes labeled with circular markers by color: red, white, and blue. Birthed from these well-labeled trails are many social paths leading across the mountainside. To create a mile-long loop begin on the red trail, heading south up the mountain from the trailhead. After just a few hundred feet you perch above the highway with the first of many dramatic views. At this point, the trail scales a steep open scree slope with a looming drop down to the Elliott Highway. The red trail will end at Twin Towers—the first of the large tors (weathered granite pinnacles).

As you encroach on Twin Towers pay close attention to the markers on the trees. The white trail forks left about 75 feet away from, and below, the towers. This white trail leads to Falcon Rock where you'll hop on the blue trail for descent. Falcon Rock has some sweeping rock-top vistas, no climbing required. On the way down the blue trail is quite steep but you can retrace the red if you're not up to the journey. The blue trail grade is very brief and levels out into a steadier decline about a quarter of the way down the descent.

Miles and Directions

0.0 Take the red trail south up the mountain from the trailhead.

0.2 Reach small rock outcropping.

0.4 Arrive at Twin Towers: Various social trails fork off. Stay left and follow red trail for 75 feet to White Trail entrance.

0.5 Reach Falcon Rock and striking views from the top. Make a slight U-turn and follow Blue Trail for descent.

0.9 Return to parking area, trailhead to left.

1.0 Arrive back at the trailhead.

8 Summit Trail to Wickersham Dome

A high alpine hike in the White Mountains National Recreation Area, this 7-mile round-trip tour winds through low-lying arctic tundra and stunted spruce and birch forests. The trip ends atop a cluster of rock outcroppings high above the treeline on Wickersham Dome. The 360-degree panoramas offer some of the best vistas of the Fairbanks area.

Distance: 7.0 miles out and back (with shorter and longer options)

Approximate hiking time: 3.5 to 5 hours

Difficulty: Moderate to challenging (challenging for some due to length)

Trail surface: Rock, dirt, boardwalk

Best season: Summer through fall

Other trail users: None

Canine compatibility: Leashed dogs permitted

Fees and permits: No fees or permits required

Schedule: None

Maps: TOPO! Alaska CD 5, USGS Livengood A-3, Bureau of Land Management leaflet Summit Trail, and brochure White Mountains National Recreation Winter Trails and Cabins.

Trail contacts: Bureau of Land Management, Fairbanks District Office, 1150 University Avenue, Fairbanks, AK 99709; (907) 474-2200, (800) 437-7021; www.blm.gov/ak

Finding the trailhead: From Fairbanks take the Steese Highway 11 miles north to the junction with the Elliott Highway in Fox. Continue north on the Elliott Highway (Route 2) for 28 miles to the Wickersham Dome trailhead on the right. The parking area is also home to the Wickersham Creek Trail, a wet winter route, located near the vault toilet. The trailhead for Summit Trail is in the northern corner of the parking lot, closer to the Elliott Highway at GPS coordinates N65 10.707' / W148 04.590'.

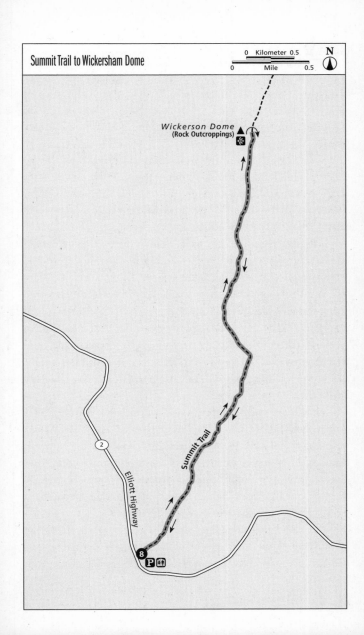

Summit Trail to Wickersham Dome

0 Kilometer 0.5
0 Mile 0.5

N

Wickerson Dome
(Rock Outcroppings)

Summit Trail

Elliott Highway

2

8

The Hike

You don't have to travel far along the Summit Trail to get that top-of-the-world feel. By an easy half mile the thickets of dwarf spruce and birch forest fade and the open mountain panorama emerges—a quick taste of the high alpine country ahead.

The whole of Summit Trail totals 20 miles one-way to Beaver Creek. The most popular tour of the route leads 7 miles out and back to a chunk of rock outcroppings on Wickersham Dome. The day hike to the rocks is so popular many refer to the trail solely as "Wickersham Dome."

For the first mile Summit Trail scurries between bald knobs and wet dwarf forest, offering some relief from the windy high points. After a mile an old boardwalk replaces the squishy soils. Due to permafrost, moisture on this trail has a tendency to puddle up and create the feel of a recent flood in lower areas. Several new sections of plank have been installed, and a plan to replace the boardwalk is in order; however, a significant amount of footing remains rickety and mangled where the permafrost has recently shifted.

The boardwalk abruptly ends a little over a mile and a half in, just before access to a winter trail (generally impassably soggy in summer) on the right. Stay left for Summit Trail and begin the ascent above the treeline. As you climb the naked hump the footing becomes rocky and completely washed out in places. At other sections wooden teepees and rock cairns mark the less noticeable route.

The last half mile offers some of the trail's best. White Mountain panoramas grab your attention as the route levels into an easy mountain–high stroll. Beautiful all summer long, the rolling arctic tundra blooms with wildflowers in June and July then fades into berries a few short weeks later. This is one of the most popular picking spots, so stop and have a few blueberries if nature allows. By mid–August fall colors crawl across the tundra like fire. At the trail's end, cairns dot the way to rock outcroppings on the left and many social trails easily lead to the top, a perfect ending location and lunching spot with a million dollar view—wind allowing. Always prepare for wind and rain on this trail. Miles of exposed mountaintops offer spectacular vistas, but provide absolutely no shelter in a storm.

Miles and Directions

0.0 Follow trail northeast from parking area.

0.5 Climbs up to wide open flat hilltop (great views if you want to bail out here for a 1-mile hike).

1.7 End boardwalk, and shortly thereafter intersect with winter trail; stay left.

3.5 Reach rock outcroppings. Rock cairns mark the main social trail to left; follow to the top of the rocks 100 yards to left for unsurpassed views.

7.0 Arrive back at the trailhead.

$\mathcal{9}$ Birch Hill's Blue Loop

With its proximity to downtown, the Birch Hill Recreation Area is practically an urban trail system. Pioneered by the Nordic Ski Club of Fairbanks, the park famously lures cross-country skiers during the snowy months. In spring the slopes melt into casual hiking routes. The easy 1.1–mile Blue Loop lightly gains elevation as it circles through the characteristically lofty birch forest.

Distance: 1.1-mile lollipop (with longer options)
Approximate hiking time: 30 minutes
Difficulty: Easy
Trail surface: Grass
Best season: Mid-April through mid-October
Other trail users: Runners, cyclists, disc golfers
Canine compatibility: Leashed dogs permitted
Fees and permits: No fees or permits required
Schedule: Open for hikers 6:00 a.m. to 10:00 p.m., April 16 through October 14.
Maps: TOPO! Alaska CD 5, USGS Fairbanks D-2, Nordic Ski Club of Fairbanks Birch Hill Nordic Ski Trails
Trail contacts: Fairbanks North Star Borough Parks and Recreation Department, 809 Pioneer Road, Fairbanks, AK 99701; (907) 459-1070; http://co.fairbanks.ak.us/ParksandRecreation; Nordic Ski Club of Fairbanks, 1540 Hayes Avenue, Fairbanks, AK 99709; (907) 474-4242; www.nscfairbanks.org
Special considerations: No foot traffic or pets permitted when trails are groomed for skiers October 15 through April 15.

Finding the trailhead: Birch Hill is just north of Fairbanks city proper. From Fairbanks take the Steese Highway north a couple miles to the Fairhill Road stoplight. Turn east onto Fairhill Road and make

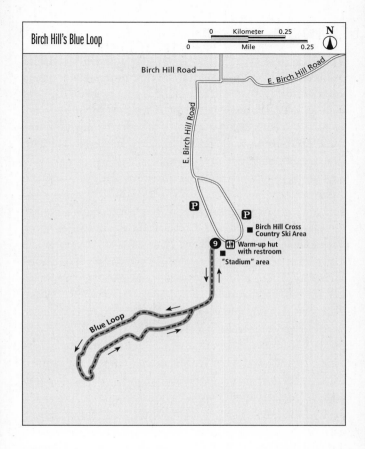

Birch Hill's Blue Loop

0   Kilometer   0.25
0   Mile   0.25

N

Birch Hill Road

E. Birch Hill Road

E. Birch Hill Road

P

P Birch Hill Cross
   Country Ski Area

9 Warm-up hut
   with restroom

"Stadium" area

Blue Loop

an immediate left onto Birch Hill Road. Follow Birch Hill Road for 2 miles and turn right onto East Birch Hill Road. Drive 0.1 mile to the parking lots and Birch Hill Cross Country Ski Center. Directions begin at GPS position N64 52.095' / W147 38.862'.

The Hike

You'll know why it's called Birch Hill when you roll into this recreation area and see the birch trees thickly encasing the road. Fall colors of the deciduous beauties, especially in such abundance, are a real treat. Close to downtown and home to a complex system of easily accessible trails, the Birch Hill Recreation Area is popular year-round, but with two exceptionally different crowds.

During winter the prestigious trails are groomed and highly regarded by skiers. The winter wonderland is limited solely to ski exploration during this time. However, the summer months produce a casual community of runners, disc golfers, and dog walkers. The wide ski slopes create super-sized hiking trails, several of which are maintained and mowed into a level grassy footing. Most of the routes are accessible in some way, though the enticing White Bear Trail is enduringly soggy. The Warm Up Loop is an easy half mile recommended for those who would like to "taste" the trails and avoid any elevation gain. One of the easiest-to-follow and best-maintained options is the popular Blue Loop, which encompasses a chunk of the disc golf course. You can begin your adventures here; take a map and explore the possibilities of other routes.

The Blue Loop trailhead is a little over 0.1 mile from the parking area. Begin at the Cross Country Ski Center, where you will also find well-maintained restrooms and drinking fountains. From the open stadium cut across to the southern corner. Follow the disc golf course up a very wide slope along a gradual hill. The Blue Loop trailhead is well labeled on the right. At just under a mile, this trail is a recommended starting point for Birch Hill explorations and travels over humble hills through slender birch groves.

Miles and Directions

0.0 Begin at the Birch Hill Cross Country Ski Center; head across the open stadium area to the southern corner.

0.1 At the southern corner, follow the disc golf course south up the hill.

0.2 Reach the top of the slope and Blue Loop trailhead to the right.

0.7 Stay left for Blue Loop return.

0.9 Return to Blue Loop trailhead.

1.0 Reach stadium.

1.1 Arrive back at the Cross Country Ski Center.

10 Table Top Mountain

Located in the heart of the White Mountains National Recreation Area, this 3-mile loop traverses through a regenerating spruce forest and crests in the rocky subalpine zone. Picture-perfect panoramas reach as far as the white peaks of the Alaska Range. Colorful early summer wildflowers and late summer fireweed blooms dazzle the eyes.

Distance: 3.0-mile loop
Approximate hiking time: 1.5 to 3 hours
Difficulty: Moderate
Trail surface: Rock, dirt
Best season: Summer
Other trail users: None
Canine compatibility: Leashed dogs permitted
Fees and permits: No fees or permits required

Schedule: None
Maps: TOPO! Alaska CD 5, USGS Circle B-6
Trail contacts: Bureau of Land Management, Fairbanks District Office, 1150 University Avenue, Fairbanks, AK 99709; (907) 474-2200, (800) 437-7021; www.blm.gov/ak
Special considerations: There are no facilities at this trailhead.

Finding the trailhead: From Fairbanks take the Steese Highway north 11 miles to Fox and the junction of the Elliott Highway. Stay on the Steese Highway to mile 57.4 and turn north onto U.S. Creek Road. Drive 7 miles, passing through the recreational panning area, and turn left onto the unlabeled gravel road, following the sign toward the Ophir Creek Campground. The Table Top Mountain trailhead is 8.4 miles down the road on the right. This loop trail joins the road a couple hundred feet apart from beginning to end. Directions follow a clockwise loop, beginning on the westernmost link of the trail, and GPS coordinates N65 21.231' / W146 58.405'.

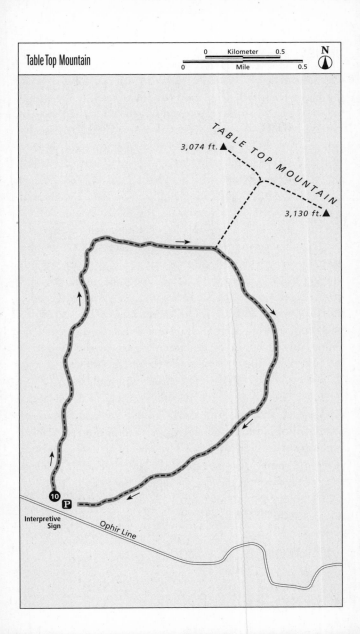

Table Top Mountain

0   Kilometer   0.5

0   Mile   0.5

N

TABLE TOP MOUNTAIN

3,074 ft. ▲

3,130 ft. ▲

10 P

Interpretive
Sign

Ophir Line

The Hike

On a clear day, you might feel you can see forever with the views from the Table Top Mountain trail. It is possible for the scene to stretch from the jagged limestone peaks of the White Mountains to the far distant snowcapped Alaska Range. A wildfire in 2004 did not take from the beauty of this landscape. Young spruce, juniper, dwarf dogwood, and waist-high grasses bring life to the once burned land. A rich woodpecker population delights in the recently charred trunks. The berry-rich south-facing slope of this mountain can host some of the region's best fall picking.

The drainage is poor as the trail begins. The footing jumps from rocky and uneven to wet and soupy in the lower elevations. Erosion control and trail restoration has begun on this route; in the meantime watch your step over the large rocks and logs. The rather steady, and therefore not overpowering, climb of around a thousand feet begins almost immediately. The trail finely zigzags up the mountain over the first mile creating a moderate climb before it levels out into scattered dwarfed spruce along the hem of the treeline. The route is etched fairly securely in the decomposing rock and soil; rock cairns ensure the way. The bald mountaintop lies directly above the trail. A few short spurs lead to two summits of Table Top Mountain about midway along the route. Around mile 2 the loop begins to descend and travels through scenery paralleling the journey up.

Be especially prepared for wind or an oncoming storm on this trail; bring plenty of layers and sunblock. Once above the treeline it can get gusty, and weather patterns change quickly.

Miles and Directions

0.0 Begin clockwise on the trail by following the trail closest to the interpretive sign.

1.5 Two short spur trails lead to the summit of Table Top Mountain.

3.0 Arrive back at the road; trailhead is 500 feet to right.

11 Pinnell Mountain Trail

Eagle Summit is located at the eastern trailhead of the Pinnell Mountain Trail two hours northeast of Fairbanks. The summit is known locally as a hot spot to view the midnight sun. A short 0.4-mile interpretive trail leads through the region's high country to sun-viewing decks, just a drop below the Arctic Circle. On your way stroll by two billion-year-old rocks, thousand-year-old lichen, and beautiful annual wildflower blooms.

Distance: 0.4-mile loop (with longer options)
Approximate hiking time: 30 minutes
Difficulty: Easy (moderate with Pinnell Mountain)
Trail surface: Gravel, rock, dirt
Best season: Summer
Other trail users: None
Canine compatibility: Leashed dogs permitted
Fees and permits: No fees or permits required
Schedule: None
Maps: TOPO! Alaska CD 5,
USGS Circle B-3, BLM brochures Eagle Summit: Window to the Midnight Sun and Pinnell Mountain National Recreation Trail
Trail contacts: Bureau of Land Management, Eastern Interior Field Office, 1150 University Avenue, Fairbanks, AK 99709; (907) 474-2200, (800) 437-7021; www.blm.gov/ak
Special considerations: Prepare for cold weather; this high arctic trail can easily dip below freezing at any time of day or year. There is no water at this trailhead.

Finding the trailhead: Access to the 27-mile Pinnell Mountain Trail can be found at either mile 85 or 107 of the Steese Highway. The Eagle Summit Wayside, which includes the interpretive loop, is located at mile 107. To reach the wayside, hop on the Steese Highway in Fairbanks and drive 11 miles to the town of Fox. Stay right

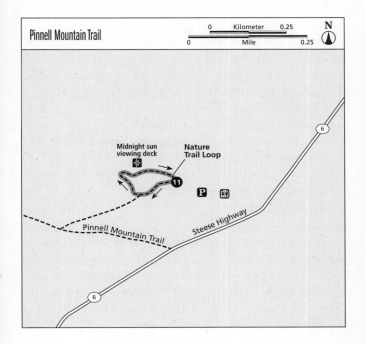

Midnight sun
viewing deck

Nature
Trail Loop

Pinnell Mountain Trail

Steese Highway

and follow the Steese Highway east 96 miles to the Eagle Summit Wayside on your left and the trailhead at GPS N65 29.070' / W145 24.977'.

The Hike

The city of Fairbanks itself is just a bit too low to view the summer's midnight sun, although it may seem like broad daylight at that time. To see the spectacular solstice sun above the horizon at the magical stroke of midnight, you'll have to make this drive two hours north of the city. The journey along the Steese Highway is an adventure on its own; you can almost feel the arctic latitude encroach as you climb into the high country. At Eagle Summit a short trail adjacent to the parking area leads to midnight sun viewing decks, where from June 17 through June 24 you can see the blazing crest above the horizon at midnight. Situated on a bare hilltop below the Pinnell Mountain Trail, the interpretive loop is a highly educational and a leisurely tundra wander, at any time of day. But for the real interior experience stock up on coffee, bring a warm jacket, and make the drive to this arctic wonderland late on a summer evening to truly indulge in the midnight sun. Or, for a special challenge hop on the Pinnell Mountain Trail for an extra half mile for a good lookout point.

The interpretive signs along the trail describe the hardy plants and wildlife that can survive in this wind-whipped arctic desert. Bring the binoculars as migrating caribou are often spotted from the trail. Also keep an eye out for other high mountain critters, including marmots, pika, and ptarmigan. If you're too late for the midnight sun, indulge in the midsummer wildflower blooms when spectacularly strong plants take advantage of their few weeks of good sun. Look for Perry's wallflower, arctic lupine, spring beauty, moss campion, and alpine azalea.

Be prepared for a moderate hike if you head up the Pinnell Mountain Trail, especially at this high elevation. In its entirety the trail extends 27 miles west and is a strenuous journey. The half-mile version however offers a nice sample of the trail as it moderately climbs a mountainside overlooking Eagle Summit. Prepare for extreme weather on either trail; at any time during the day or summer the temperature can be freezing and snow can linger to July.

Miles and Directions

0.0 Begin loop.

0.1 Reach Pinnell Mountain Trail access in loop's southwest corner.

0.4 Arrive back at the parking area.

12 Fairbanks–Circle Historical Trail

This historical gold–rush route once connected the miners of Circle City to the supply post of Fairbanks. Today the rugged trail is accessible at several points along the Steese Highway and creates attractive easy day hikes. Some of the most scenic portions stretch through the high alpine tundra of the Twelvemile Wayside area.

Distance: 2.0 miles out and back (with longer options)
Approximate hiking time: 1 hour
Difficulty: Moderate
Trail surface: Dirt, rock
Best season: Summer
Other trail users: Motorized vehicles
Canine compatibility: Leashed pets permitted
Fees and permits: No fees or permits required
Schedule: None

Maps: TOPO! Alaska CD 5, USGS Circle B-4.
Trail contacts: Alaska Department of Natural Resources, Fairbanks Area Office, 3700 Airport Way, Fairbanks, AK 99709; (907) 451-2601; www.dnr.state .ak.us
Special considerations: Motorized vehicles are permitted on this trail. There are no amenities or facilities at this trailhead. This trail is not officially maintained.

Finding the trailhead: You can pick up the Fairbanks–Circle Historical Trail at the Twelvemile Wayside opposite of the Pinnell Mountain Trail at mile 85.5 of the Steese Highway. From Fairbanks take the Steese Highway north 11 miles to the town of Fox. Stay right and follow the Steese Highway east 74 miles to the wayside on your right and trailhead at GPS coordinates N65 23.493' / W145 58.368'.

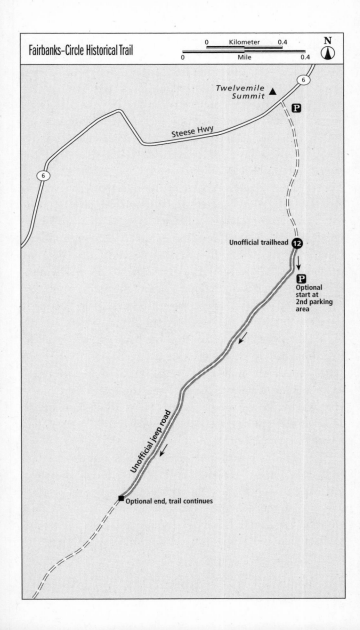

The Hike

In the late 1800s this route linked the supply post of Fairbanks to Circle City and the booming Circle Mining District. The Fairbanks–Circle Historical Trail was somewhat short lived and was replaced by the Steese Highway in the 1920s. The Circle Mining District, however, remains active both commercially and recreationally and has produced over a million ounces of gold.

There are several sections of the trail that can make an easy day hike. For a scenic trip through the high country, the Twelvemile Wayside allows access to the Fairbanks–Circle Historical Trail from the Pinnell Mountain trailhead. Here you can park at the primitive wayside (no amenities) and hop on the southern route opposite the Pinnell Mountain Trail, which is on the north side of the Steese Highway. The trail begins at a sign close to the entrance, but many people will park at the back parking lot at mile 0.3 of the hike. Once you hike away from the back parking area, the trail immediately climbs up a small knoll to a nice outlook after a moderate mile-long climb. From there a forested valley lies farther down the trail and the span of the Steese Highway stretches to the north. Here you'll find tundra as far as the eye can see, low-growing brush, berries, and dwarfed flower blooms.

The trail is open to motorized vehicles, but it is a rough road even for a jeep. Most motorized traffic is limited to small all-terrain vehicles, but with the exception of productive late summer berry-picking weekends, traffic is rare. Hunting also accounts for late summer and early fall motorized activity, so be especially cautious during this time.

Miles and Directions

0.0 Begin at the Twelvemile Wayside. The trailhead is closer to the Steese Highway, but many will scrape 0.3 mile off the hike by hopping on the trail from the back parking lot.

0.3 Intersection with road and parking area to left.

1.0 End at top of knob.

2.0 Arrive back at the trailhead.

13 Two Rivers Ski Trails

A cousin to Birch Hill, the less often visited Two Rivers Ski Trails host quiet summer hikes through a breezy birch forest. The wide level hikes pass through giant birch groves on mowed grassy paths. Options range from 0.6- to 4.7-mile loops.

Distance: 1.5-mile loop (with shorter and longer options)
Approximate hiking time: 45 minutes
Difficulty: Easy
Trail surface: Dirt, grass
Best season: Summer through fall
Other trail users: Runners, cyclists, horses
Canine compatibility: Leashed dogs permitted
Fees and permits: No fees or permits required
Schedule: Groomed for skiers and skijoring in winter months
Maps: TOPO! Alaska CD 5, Fair-banks D-1

Trail contacts: Fairbanks North Star Borough Parks and Recreation Department, 809 Pioneer Road, Fairbanks, AK 99701; (907) 459-1070; http://co.fairbanks.ak.us/ParksandRecreation; Nordic Ski Club of Fairbanks, 1540 Hayes Avenue, Fairbanks, AK 99709; (907) 474-4242; www.nscfairbanks.org
Special considerations: Nordic Ski Club volunteers maintain these trails. The trail status could change at any time. There are no facilities at this trailhead.

Finding the trailhead: From Fairbanks take the Steese Highway a few miles north to mile 4.9 and exit east onto Chena Hot Springs Road. Follow Chena Hot Springs Road 18.4 miles and turn left onto Two Rivers Road. Drive 0.5 mile and turn right at the sign for Two Rivers Ski/Hike Trails. You will see the Two Rivers Elementary School on the right and the trailhead on your left at GPS coordinates N64

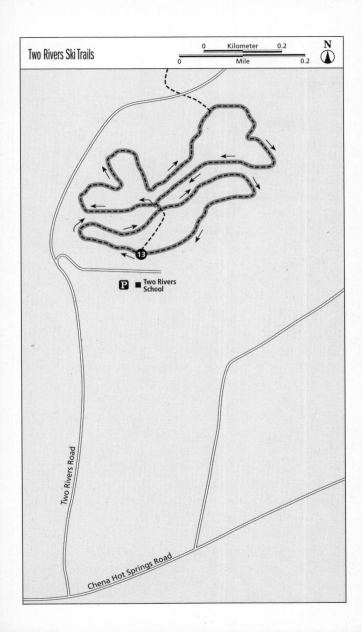

Two Rivers Ski Trails

0   Kilometer   0.2

0   Mile   0.2

N

13

P ■ Two Rivers
    School

Two Rivers Road

Chena Hot Springs Road

52.670' / W147 02.334'. Drive around the loop to the parking area in front of the school.

The Hike

The looping ski trails in the boreal forest behind the Two Rivers Elementary School are run by a collaborative effort between the Fairbanks North Star Borough and volunteers of the Nordic Ski Club of Fairbanks. Similar to Birch Hill, the trails are desirable winter ski routes that offer easy summer hiking. Though not nearly as prestigious or well maintained as Birch Hill, Two Rivers also doesn't get much traffic and unless the school just concluded for the day you're likely to be the only one playing on these trails.

The system has several interconnecting loops that can be linked in figure-eight-style options. To create a longer route, always combine the trail before it. Options include 1k (0.6 mile), 2.5k (1.5 mile), 5k (3.1 mile), and 7.5k (4.7 mile) loops. You can use any loop during the summer, but be aware in the farthest, 7.5k loop, you'll find steep grades and due to less traffic the trail is not as well maintained in summer. There is also a longer out-and-back horse trail option.

The easiest to follow and most well-traveled summer trails are the 1k and 2.5k loops, detailed in this book. To begin, be sure to stop by the trailhead and study the sign for a minute to catch your bearings, then head west on the lowest trail (this will be the 1k loop, labeled 1, 2.5 and 7.5k). At an intersection about 0.3k in, take the backwards Y to follow the 2.5k, or follow the sign straight ahead for the 1k. These easy trails can be confusing as you get to know them, but have minimal grade.

All of the trails loop through an enduringly tall birch forest. The extra-wide sloped paths are primarily mowed but sometimes in a lengthy cut. The breezy hillside dries out quickly, creating a dry trail fairly early in the summer season. Classic boreal forest critters including moose, squirrels, and birds are easily spotted on these quiet trails.

Miles and Directions

0.0 Begin at trailhead and head west on the lowest trail.

0.2 Intersection with shortcut to trailhead to right (bail out for a half-mile stroll); stay left then follow backwards Y (unlabeled coming from your direction) for 2.5k hike.

1.0 Intersection with 5k and 7.5k to left, stay right for 2.5k.

1.3 Merge onto 1k for return.

1.5 Arrive back at the trailhead.

14 Granite Tors 2-Mile Loop

Granite Tors is traditionally a strenuous 15-mile trek showcasing granite pinnacles high in the alpine zone. The revamped addition of an easy 2-mile loop to the trail offers an excellent alternative to the challenging haul. With distant views of the tors, the 2-mile loop stretches along the North Fork Chena River and diverts through vast burn patches that enable spanning vistas despite low elevations.

Distance: 2.1-mile lollipop (with longer options)
Approximate hiking time: 1 hour
Difficulty: Moderate
Trail surface: Dirt, boardwalk
Best season: Summer
Other trail users: None
Canine compatibility: Leashed dogs permitted
Fees and permits: Day use fee
Schedule: None
Maps: TOPO! Alaska CD 5, USGS Big Delta D-5, Alaska

State Parks leaflet Granite Tors Trail
Trail contacts: Alaska State Parks, Northern Area Office, 3700 Airport Way, Fairbanks, AK 99709; (907) 451-2695; www .dnr.state.ak.us/parks
Special considerations: This route is sometimes labeled and referred to as the "3-mile Loop" although the mileage is closer to 2 miles.

Finding the trailhead: From Fairbanks take the Steese Highway a few miles north to mile 4.9 and exit east onto Chena Hot Springs Road. Drive 39 miles down Chena Hot Springs Road and turn left into the Granite Tors trailhead and campground at mile 39.4, just over the North Fork Chena River Bridge. Park in the large well-developed parking area near the gravel pit. Here you will find a pic-nicking area, restrooms, and water. Begin the trail at the interpretive sign on the south end of the parking lot at GPS coordinates N64 54.164' / W146 21.807'.

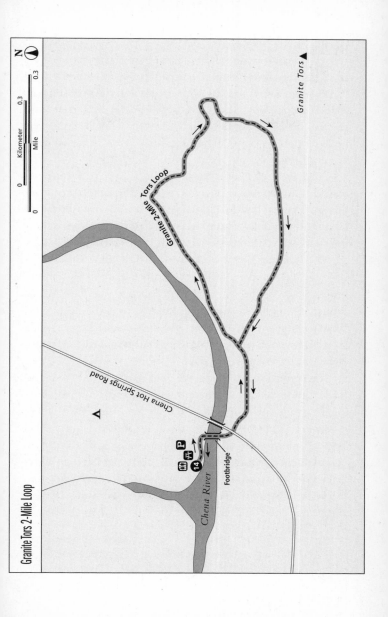

Granite Tors 2-Mile Loop

The Hike

In its entirety, the 15-mile Granite Tors Trail climbs a steep 2,700 feet, cresting on bare mountains and meandering past unique granite outcrops (tors) carved by the wind, rain, and snow. This route could be hiked in a day, but it would not be described as "easy." The strenuous trek is generally broken into two days by hikers, who backpack in.

For Best Easy Day Hikers, Granite Tors also features an easy 2-mile loop that offers a taste of the rugged territory but on an easy grade. Although the 2-mile loop does not climb to the alpine country, it passes through handsome lush forest and offers distant views of the pinnacles.

The loop can be traveled in either direction. Most hikers who set out to accomplish the Granite Tors in its entirety head clockwise in the direction labeled the East Ridge Route, through a steadier ascent, rather than the steep West Valley route. For this reason, the directions for the 2-mile loop are given in a clockwise manner although the elevation change is minimal either way.

After you join the loop the trail narrows into a single-track path through a regenerating boggy spruce forest, skirting alongside the North Fork Chena River for spells where the sweet sounds of the rushing water join the quiet hike. Several interpretive signs on flora, fauna, and ecosystems complement this loop. A few small footbridges detour hikers from the river over accompanying streams and deeper into the forest where fireweed, cotton grass, mushrooms, berries, and moss lichens find life in the burn patches, a demonstration of how fire is part of the natural environment.

Miles and Directions

0.0 Begin at trailhead and parking area; follow metal footbridge across Chena River.

0.1 Cautiously cross the guardrails and Chena Hot Springs Road; follow trail east along river, past the gauging station.

0.2 Intersection with loop and sign; go left for the East Ridge Route.

0.5 View of tors on the mountainside in distance to right.

0.9 Granite Tors Trail straight ahead; go right for 2-mile loop.

1.2 Intersection with trail, stay right for 2-mile loop.

1.8 Return to beginning of loop.

2.0 Cross road.

2.1 Arrive back at the trailhead.

15 Angel Rocks

Poking out above the miles thick and miles wide Chena Hot Springs pluton are the uniquely shaped granite and basalt formations of Angel Rocks. Perched on heavenly ledges above the boreal forest, in the wildflower-ridden subalpine zone, the rocks are a dramatic sight. The 3.5-mile Angel Rocks loop is one of the most popular hikes in the Fairbanks area. An additional 8-mile trail leads hikers to the Chena Hot Springs Resort.

Distance: 3.5-mile lollipop (with longer options)
Approximate hiking time: 2 to 4 hours
Difficulty: Moderate (with short, but challenging, grade near Angel Rocks)
Trail surface: Rock, gravel, dirt
Best season: Summer
Other trail users: Horses
Canine compatibility: Leashed dogs permitted
Fees and permits: Day use fee
Schedule: None
Maps: TOPO! Alaska CD 5; USGS Circle A-5, Alaska State Parks leaflet Angel Rocks Trail
Trail contacts: Alaska State Parks, Northern Area Office, 3700 Airport Way, Fairbanks, AK 99709; (907) 451-2695; www .dnr.state.ak.us/parks

Finding the trailhead: From Fairbanks take the Steese Highway a few miles north to mile 4.9 and exit east onto Chena Hot Springs Road. Follow Chena Hot Springs Road 48.9 miles and turn right, just over the North Fork Chena River Bridge, to the parking area. Find the trailhead at GPS coordinates N65 00.606' / W146 13.045'. The well-developed trailhead also has nearly new facilities including a beautiful waterfront picnic area and clean vault toilets.

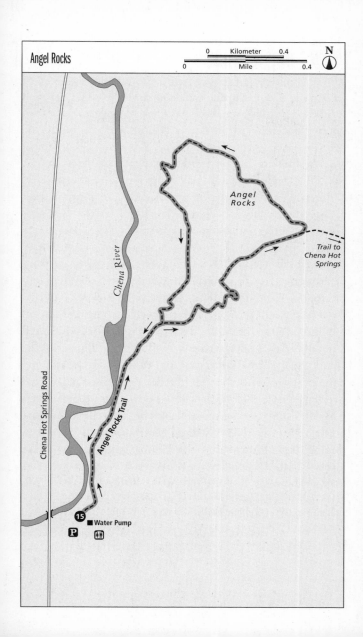

The Hike

The 3.5-mile Angel Rocks trail is the premier day hike of Fairbanks. The beautiful rock pinnacles that have eroded from the soft soils over millions of years fascinate and inspire hikers throughout the summer season; you are rarely the only one indulging in the terrain. The Angel Rocks trail leads to similarly intriguing outcroppings as the Granite Tors and Quartz Creek Trails but doesn't require the physical endurance or the hiking time to reach the rock formations.

Recently renovated and well labeled, Angel Rocks is dotted by brown markers and fresh-cut steps. Begin the trail at the interpretive signs. When you've updated your naturalist knowledge, follow the paved path northeast from the parking area. In a couple hundred feet the entrance to the loop will be on your left and there is a water pump at your right—an excellent place to water the dog and top off the bottles. From there the wide gravel path moves through a mature spruce and birch forest aside the shallow rushing North Fork Chena River. Almost immediately weathering boulders peer out of the lush hillsides along the trail. In a tad over half a mile the out-and-back portion of the hike meets with the loop; head counterclockwise. This lower-leveled portion of the trail travels along boardwalks and an earthen singletrack path through a regenerating spruce forest as the ascent begins. Once scarred by fire, the fresh green branches now promisingly find life out of the blackened spruce and fireweed patches. From here you can peer at Angel Rocks on the mountainside above.

The trail gains considerable ground as the pinnacles come into closer range. Although the 900-foot gain in elevation is divided among switchbacks, this portion of the trail can be a cardio challenge for some. The first of the Angel Rocks is met at a little over a mile as the main trail begins to crest along a rocky ridge. The hike levels out and is strewn between various pinnacles. A labeled route to the right leads 8.3 miles one way to the Chena Hot Springs Resort. There are also plenty of opportunities to explore several social trails leading to individual rocks and sweeping overlooks. This is an excellent place to stop and have lunch and possibly spy a raptor. Wildflowers can also be seen throughout the summer soaking up the cool wind and sun of this subalpine zone. Beautiful pink bursts of moss campion and purple arctic lupine, mountain harebell, and even the bright yellow Alaska poppies find life on these peaks.

Upon return the first descent has slippery decomposed granite footings that may be a bit tricky for some hikers, but quickly evens out into a gradual slope as it reaches the cool thick spruce forest below. On this return the shaded path wanders by sloughs and some of the largest beaver dams in the area. Along with these paddling aquatic favorites you may come across chattering squirrels, chirping warblers, and belted kingfishers.

Miles and Directions

0.0 Begin hiking northeast away from the interpretive signs along the paved walkway that leads 200 feet to a water pump (on right) and the gravel Angel Rocks Trail (left).

0.6 The out-and-back portion of the trail meets with the Angel Rocks loop and trail sign; follow the sign right for a counter-clockwise loop.

0.7 Intersection with horse route; stay right for Angel Rocks.

1.5 At the center of the leveled-out ridge, the 3-mile loop intersects with the Angel Rocks–Chena Hot Springs trail to right. Stay left for the 3-mile Angel Rocks loop.

2.8 Intersection with horse loop; stay right for Angel Rocks loop.

2.9 Loop ends at return to the out-and-back portion of the trail; go right.

3.5 Arrive back at the trailhead.

16 Monument Creek Trail

The historic Chena Hot Springs Resort is home to an impressive array of trails. The Monument Creek Trail is an easy hike that wraps around a small creek and links most other trailheads at the resort. The 3-mile loop can be extended or shortened with a mile-long interpretive Nature Trail, where year-round dogsled teams tour.

Distance: 3.3-mile loop (with shorter and longer options)
Approximate hiking time: 2 hours
Difficulty: Easy
Trail surface: Gravel, dirt
Best season: Spring through fall
Other trail users: Runners, cyclists, horses, dog-teams
Canine compatibility: Leashed pets permitted
Fees and permits: No fees or permits required
Schedule: Open year-round, prepare for snow October through May.

Maps: TOPO! Alaska CD 5, Chena Hot Springs Resort trail leaflet
Trail contacts: Chena Hot Springs Resort, P.O. Box 58740, Fairbanks, AK 99711; (907) 451-8104; www.chenahotsprings .com
Special considerations: This is private property. Pets are permitted on trails and in the campgrounds; they are not permitted in the lodge or other resort facilities. Be sure to stop by the Activities Center for a free copy of the resort's trail map.

Finding the trailhead: From Fairbanks take the Steese Highway a few miles north to mile 4.9 and exit east onto Chena Hot Springs Road. Follow Chena Hot Springs Road to its dead-end after 56.6 miles at the resort. Begin the trail at GPS N65 03.280' / W146 03.545'.

Monument Creek Trail

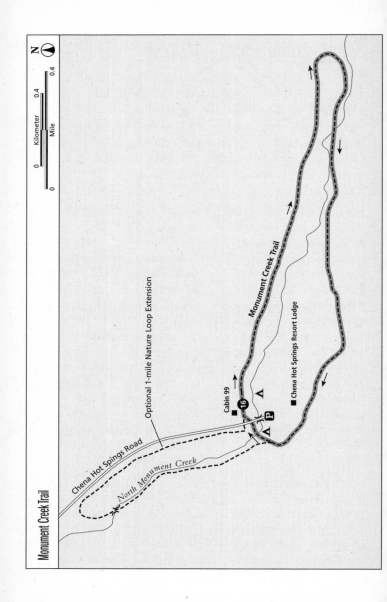

The Hike

From family-friendly nature strolls, to exhilarating climbs, the eco-friendly Chena Hot Springs Resort has a little something for everyone. The hot springs were developed in the early 1900s, when weary prospectors would take advantage of the hot mineral pools. No fees or permits are required to use the trail system, but a trip out to "Chena" without a dip in the springs would make for an incomplete adventure. The relaxing mineral pools are the perfect remedy for sore hiking limbs. It is a pleasure not to be missed.

The Monument Creek Trail is not a perfect loop; beginning at the Upper Campground, it concludes at the Lower Campground at the center of the resort. You can make it a complete loop by returning to the trailhead, but the odds are that the resort's amenities will detour your direct return. The trailhead can be found along Chena Hot Springs Road across the creek from the Upper Campground. It is not immediately labeled Monument Creek Trail, but instead you'll see a sign for FAR MTN TRAIL/CABIN 99.

Begin by walking over the bridge and following the extra-wide gravel trail east.

The scene quickly morphs into classic interior wilderness and boreal forest. Evergreens and deciduous groves transition along the crystalline creek. There are some nice valley views along Monument Creek, especially considering that this route does not gain elevation. Keep an eye out for some of the many moose who take advantage of the geothermal activity of the resort property. The moose enjoy grazing on the grass at the bottom of the pools, especially since some of the ponds do not freeze in the colder months.

The footing switches from gravel to large river rock

about halfway through after you cross an old footbridge. By 2 miles you'll pass by a landing strip where scenic flights take off daily. Near the return, the route veers from the creek and passes behind the stables, and past numerous trailheads. It then ends at the Lower Campground. From here there is an option to hop on the looping Nature Trail.

Miles and Directions

0.0 Begin along Chena Hot Springs Road at trailhead across the creek from the campground, labeled FAR MTN TRAIL/CABIN 99. Follow the trail east along the creek.

1.7 Cross the old footbridge; trail footing is large river rocks.

2.4 Merge with maintenance road; stay right, then left, avoiding the stables.

2.6 Resort access trails to right, opposing trailheads to left; stay straight for Monument Creek Trail.

2.7 Trail to left leads to aurorium (building for viewing the northern lights).

2.9 Pass outdoor hot springs pools to right.

3.0 Cross over creek and enter yurts/cabins/Lower Campground. You have an option to stay on the trail and head left on the 1-mile Nature Trail, head to the resort facilities, or cut straight across the parking areas and return to the trailhead.

3.3 Arrive back at the trailhead.

17 Chena River Nature Trail

Chena Lakes Recreation Area is a bustling weekend destination just twenty minutes from Fairbanks. Despite the crowds, the Chena River Nature Trail is something of an unspoiled gem tucked away in a forested corner of the park. Accompanied by an excellent interpretive guide, nature lovers will experience a great day hike on this older earthy trail passing through a variety of phases of boreal forest succession.

Distance: 2.5-mile loop (with shorter options)
Approximate hiking time: 1.5 hours
Difficulty: Easy
Trail surface: Dirt
Best season: Spring through fall
Other trail users: Runners, cyclists
Canine compatibility: Leashed dogs permitted
Fees and permits: Day use fee

Schedule: None
Maps: TOPO! Alaska CD 5, USGS Fairbanks D-1, Fairbanks North Star Borough pamphlet Chena River Nature Trail
Trail contacts: Fairbanks North Star Borough Parks and Recreation Department, 809 Pioneer Road, Fairbanks, AK 99701; (907) 459-1070; http://co.fair banks.ak.us/ParksandRecreation

Finding the trailhead: From Fairbanks take the Richardson Highway south about 15 miles and exit north onto Laurance Road at mile 346.7. Drive 2.6 miles to the park fee kiosk (ask for a copy of the nature guide) in Chena Lakes State Recreation Area. From the kiosk drive 2.3 miles (passing Lake Park) and turn left at the unlabeled road at the sign for River Park. Drive 0.8 mile to River Side Pavilion and the trailhead at GPS N64 47.719' / W147 11.754'.

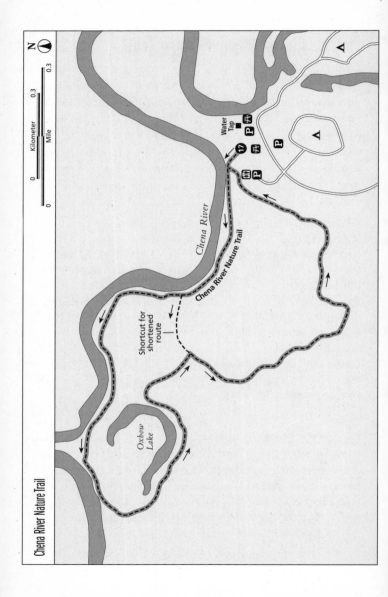

Chena River Nature Trail

Chena River

Chena River Nature Trail

Water Tap

17

P

P

P

Shortcut for shortened route

Oxbow Lake

N

Kilometer
0   0.3

Mile
0   0.3

The Hike

Chena Lakes Recreation Area is a mainstream weekend getaway for Fairbanks residents, but don't let the swarm of people, eighty campsites, or massive parking areas detour you from this nature trail. The hike is relatively unknown to beachgoers, lightly trafficked and tucked away behind picnicking grounds in the River Park section of the recreation area. The trail begins at the River Side Pavilion where you'll find restrooms, water, and a covered picnic pavilion with a map of the trail. Follow the tangle of footpaths west from the pavilion and eventually you'll catch the trail closest to the river.

An excellent (and free!) twenty-page nature trail guide details the flora, fauna, and geology of the hike. The write-ups are designed to correspond to numbers on posts, but the posts are absent. It's not too terribly important since this trail describes phases of boreal forest succession. Succession is the natural transition involving replacement of one plant community by another in an area over time. Most communities are easily identified.

The hike begins along the Chena River in an aviary-like birch grove chirping with chickadees. You might notice the peeled bark along the trees at about hand level. This bark has not been taken by wildlife, unless you count the human sorts. Peeling bark is harmful to the trees and makes them more susceptible to disease. Throughout the trail the edges are crawling in wild rose, particularly in May when the pink petals decorate the trail. Later in the season other wildflowers put on a show with fireweed, Siberian aster, dwarf dogwood, northern bedstraw, larkspur, and numerous wild berries including highbush cranberry and wild raspberry.

About a half mile down the trail there is an option to take a shortcut labeled SKI LOOP and create a 1-mile hike. The trail would continue to circle the birch grove in that instance. On the longer loop there is a stronger transition to nature. Through tall grasses, the overgrown singletrack path moves by hefty white spruce. Willow thickets take over as you move near an oxbow lake—look for muskrats and a variety of waterfowl. Moose are common in the nearby oxbow meadow. On this portion of the hike chattering squirrels are likely the only other trail users. You can feel much farther than a mile from a road, until a jet roars by every so often to remind you that you are in Fairbanks.

Miles and Directions

- **0.0** Begin at trailhead.
- **0.4** Trail fork to left is ski trail/short loop. Stay right for longer loop.
- **0.7** Blockade on trail due to previous erosion; follow new trail left.
- **1.5** Pass the other end of shortcut loop.
- **2.0** Intersection with ski trail; stay left for Nature Trail.
- **2.2** Trail parallels road, accesses restrooms.
- **2.5** Arrive back at the trailhead.

18 Beaver Slough Nature Trail

This easy self-guided nature trail wanders along placid Beaver Slough. Hikers transcend into wilderness a hop, skip, and jump away from family-friendly North Pole and the premier attractions at the Santa Claus House. The easy mile-long trail hosts interpretive signs, an old homestead cabin rendition, and a flower-enriched peace garden. As you wander along the lush slough, keep your eyes peeled for beavers!

Distance: 1 mile out and back
Approximate hiking time: 45 minutes
Difficulty: Easy
Trail surface: Gravel, dirt
Best season: Best spring through fall
Other trail users: Runners
Canine compatibility: Leashed dogs permitted
Fees and permits: No fees or permits required
Schedule: None
Maps: TOPO! Alaska CD 5, USGS Fairbanks D-1
Trail contacts: City of North Pole, Department of Public Works, 125 Snowman Lane, North Pole, AK 99705; (907) 488-8593 ext. 5054; www.north polealaska.com

Finding the trailhead: From Fairbanks take the Richardson Highway south about 12 miles to the city of North Pole. Exit south onto Badger Road/Santa Claus Lane at mile 349.7, drive 0.3 miles, and turn east onto Kevin's Way. The trailhead is on the right 0.1 mile down Kevin's Way across from the old trappers' cabin at GPS N64 45.238' / W147 21.037'.

The Hike

This impressive little nature trail follows Beaver Slough through humbling old-growth spruce forest rich with wild-

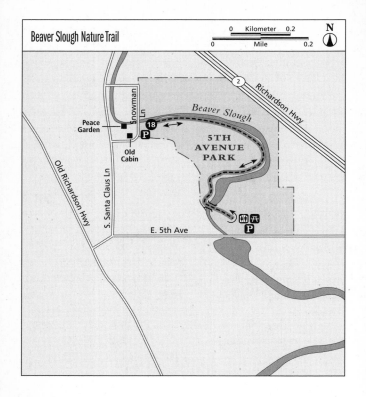

Beaver Slough Nature Trail

0   Kilometer   0.2

0   Mile   0.2

N

Richardson Hwy

(2)

Beaver Slough

Snowman Ln

Peace Garden

18

P

Old Cabin

5TH AVENUE PARK

Old Richardson Hwy

S. Santa Claus Ln

E. 5th Ave

P

flowers in downtown North Pole. The trail leads east of the parking area, but before heading out, stop by the rendition of a 1944 wilderness homestead located across the street from the trailhead. A placard at the cabin describes the history of the first legal plots in the area, the birth of the city, and the Christmas-inspired city name (hint: it does involve toys!). Next to the cabin a peace garden hosts benches and wildflower planters—one of the many Eagle Scout projects that enrich the trail.

The various interpretive signs along the way discuss the nature of the slough. Not surprisingly, beaver activity is high in this area. If you are interested in beaver viewing, arrive closer to dawn or dusk (though depending on the time of year it may be hard to decipher by the light!) when the creatures are more active. As you follow the hike notice the many dams built by these busy-bodied aquatic mammals. Sounds of ducks, red squirrels, woodpeckers, and the quiet trickle of the slough accompany the hike—so do occasional spurts of highway noise.

The trail ends after a half mile at a small city park on 5th Avenue. You can retrace the hike from the park back to the trailhead or stop and enjoy the facilities, which include shady picnic tables, restrooms, and a playground. It is possible to push to the park and back in less than half an hour, but to truly enjoy the well-developed trail allow a minimum of 45 minutes for the hike. Stop for quiet breaks at the beautiful wildlife viewing decks and take time to read all the signs. Better yet, allow two hours and take a contemplative break at the small peace garden adjacent to the old trappers' cabin. Imagine life in a rustic one-room shelter seventy years ago in Santa's town.

Miles and Directions

0.0 Begin walking east from the trailhead.
0.5 End at 5th Avenue Park, backtrack from here.
1.0 Arrive back at the trailhead.

19 Harding Lake Nature Trail

The simple 0.5-mile nature trail of the Harding Lake State Recreation Area hosts quiet wildlife viewing and a horde of red squirrels. A more rustic mile-long extension through the old-growth spruce forest can be tacked on for a longer hike.

Distance: 0.5-mile loop (with longer option)
Approximate hiking time: 30 minutes to 1 hour
Difficulty: Easy
Trail surface: Dirt
Best season: Summer
Other trail users: None
Canine compatibility: Leashed dogs permitted
Fees and permits: Daily use fee

Schedule: None
Maps: TOPO! Alaska CD 5, USGS Big Delta B-6
Trail contacts: Alaska State Parks, Northern Area Office, 3700 Airport Way, Fairbanks, AK 99709; (907) 451-2695; www .dnr.state.ak.us/parks
Special considerations: This trail was not labeled in 2008.

Finding the trailhead: From Fairbanks take the Richardson Highway 45 miles south to mile 321.6 and turn east onto Harding Drive at the sign for the Harding Lake State Recreation Area. Drive 1.5 miles to the campground entrance and fee station. Follow signs left (north) to the parking area for the walk-in tent sites/trailhead. The nature trail leads southeast into the forest aside a well-labeled trailhead located at GPS coordinates N64 26.262' / W146 52.481'. If you would like to view the map, it's posted in the large bulletin box by the water pump across from the trailhead.

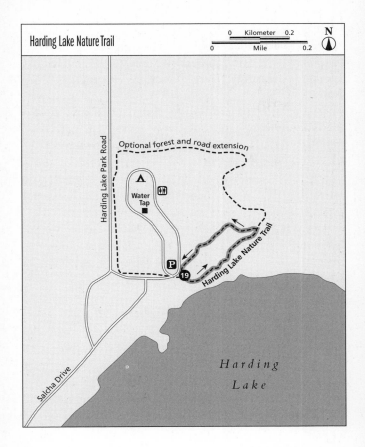

Optional forest and road extension

Harding Lake Park Road

Water Tap

Harding Lake Nature Trail

19

Salcha Drive

Harding Lake

The Hike

Less polished than other area nature trails, the Harding Lake Nature Trail also has less traffic and is likely to seem abandoned if it's not a busy camping weekend. The nature trail does not lead to the lake, but instead meanders through a moist old-growth spruce forest. The easy 0.5-mile loop is designed to have interpretive signs to complement the hike. In 2008 the signs were absent, with only empty posts visible, but there are plans to replace the displays for the upcoming season.

The nature trail leads southeast into the forest. Tangles of primitive social trails meet after a couple hundred feet and lead through willow and alder thickets toward the water. Stay left for the nature trail, which borders a quagmire before hitting the spruce forest. The wide gravel path eventually slims into a single-file trail with the occasional snagging spruce roots strewn across.

Many busy-bodied little creatures are working in this forest. Among the fat trunks of trees, check the mossy forest floor for massive squirrel middens. The brown piles of spruce cone shards are the stockpiled meals of the red squirrel. These squirrel caches are some of the largest that can be seen in the area. Do not disturb the critters hard at work; their survival depends on it. Woodpeckers also relish this old growth forest. With a surplus of aging trees, there is no shortage of snags to pluck bark beetles from. Between mile 0.3 and 0.5, squirrel and woodpecker activity abounds.

If you hop off the Harding Lake Nature Trail and onto the unlabeled route to Harding Lake Park Road, you'll find the trail more secluded and a bit less level. There is an option to use this extension as an out-and-back hike or loop by walking along the road back to the campground entrance. The lesser-used trail continues in the spruce forest skirting the back of several campsites and eventually hits Harding Lake Park Road, where you can retrace the pavement to the trailhead or retrace the hike.

Miles and Directions

0.0 Head southeast from the trailhead into the forest; after 175 feet stay left at intersection with trail.

0.2 Intersection with old road (path directly from parking area to walk-in tent sites). You can continue on nature trail or use this bailout or extension point. To bail out follow path left to parking area. To continue on nature trail follow trail markers straight ahead. To extend the trail to Harding Lake Park Road, go right and follow the trail markers next to the restroom and the trail to the road.

0.3 Pass woodpecker trees and massive squirrel middens.

0.5 Arrive back at the end of the trail; parking area is to left.

1.0 mile extension:

0.0 Begin at trailhead on Nature Trail.

0.2 Intersect with old trail; at trail marker arrow stay left.

0.5 Intersection with Harding Road; go left (south).

0.8 Campground entrance; go left (east).

1.0 Arrive back at the trailhead.

20 Quartz Lake Loop

The Quartz Lake State Recreation Area is a fun place to spend a weekend. It is home to two beautiful campgrounds, a good boating and fishing lake, and a half dozen hiking trails. The popular Quartz Lake Loop Trail travels 1.8 miles through a thick forest from the Quartz Lake Campground past an old cabin to the Lost Lake Campground. Upon return the trail ribbons scenic Quartz Lake—keep an eye out for berries and bears!

Distance: 1.8-mile loop (with shorter and longer options)
Approximate hiking time: 1 hour
Difficulty: Easy
Trail surface: Dirt
Best season: Summer through fall
Other trail users: Runners, cyclists
Canine compatibility: Leashed dogs permitted

Fees and permits: Daily use fee
Schedule: None
Maps: TOPO! Alaska CD 6, Alaska State Parks brochure Trail Guide: Quartz Lake State Recreation Area
Trail contacts: Alaska State Parks, Northern Area Office, 3700 Airport Way, Fairbanks, AK 99709; (907) 451-2695; www .dnr.state.ak.us/parks

Finding the trailhead: The Quartz Lake State Recreation Area is about an hour and a half from Fairbanks. Take the Richardson Highway south from Fairbanks 85 miles to mile 277.9 and turn north onto Quartz Lake Road. Drive 2.4 miles to the Quartz Lake Campground where the trail begins directly across from the entrance to the campground loop. If you are visiting for day use, park at the boat launch where you will find restrooms and water. Find the trailhead at GPS N64 11.852' / W145 49.743'.

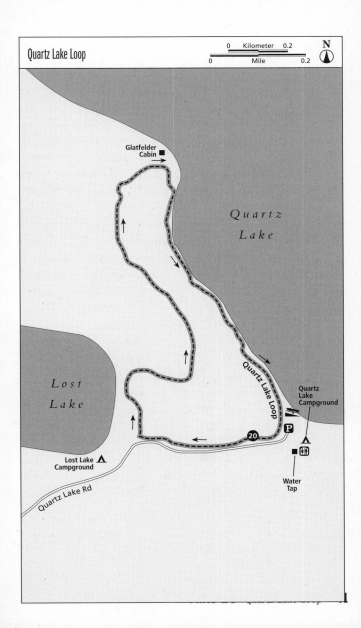

Quartz Lake Loop

0   Kilometer   0.2
0   Mile   0.2

N

Glatfelder Cabin

Quartz Lake

Quartz Lake Loop

Quartz Lake Campground

Lost Lake

20

P

Lost Lake Campground

Quartz Lake Rd

Water Tap

The Hike

The Quartz Lake State Recreation Area has several unique hiking trails, from family-friendly easy grade strolls to breathtaking marches up to Bluff Point. The 1.8-mile stretch along the Quartz Lake Loop is the most traveled of the series. The trail begins adjacent to wetland-like Quartz Lake. The mushy muskeg of the area can flood quite easily and therefore creates a mosquito haven very early and late in the season. Be sure to stock up on bug spray before your journey.

The earthen singletrack trail moves quickly through a mixed spruce forest. Here you'll find horsetails and other grasses below the trees along with early summer wildflower blooms. After a rolling mile along a pine needle path through green spruce groves, the trail reaches Glatfelder Cabin. The original cabin was built in 1956 on the five-acre homestead that predated this piece of state land. Today, the cabin has been rebuilt and is available for public use. Overlooking the lake on a forested bluff, the hike-in cabin would make for a picture perfect experience of camping at Quartz Lake; contact Alaska State Parks for more information.

To continue on Quartz Lake Loop, go right after the cabin, heading south through the brush toward Quartz Lake. The trail slowly descends to the water and skirts the shore in the final half mile. As you wander by the lake, check the surrounding bushes for wild raspberries. Be bear aware while on this trail system; there are numerous bears in this area.

Miles and Directions

0.0 Begin the trail opposite the entrance to the Quartz Lake Campground; after 150 feet follow the trail left.

0.5 Intersection with road; stay right for loop trail.

0.6 Stay right at intersection with Lost Lake Campground access road.

0.7 Intersection with Lost Lake Campground and a water pump, stay left on a wide gravel path.

0.8 Intersection with Lost Lake Trailhead; stay right for Quartz Lake Loop, or for an extension.

1.0 Reach Glatfelder Cabin; go right for Quartz Lake Loop.

1.6 Arrive at boat launch and parking area; trailhead is to right 0.2 mile ahead.

1.8 Arrive back at the trailhead.

Clubs and Trail Groups

Fairbanks Area Hiking Club
P.O. Box 80954
Fairbanks, AK 99708
(907) 455-7557

Friends of Creamer's Field
P.O. Box 81065
Fairbanks, AK 99708
(907) 452-5162

Nordic Ski Club of Fairbanks
1540 Hayes Avenue
Fairbanks, AK 99709
(907) 474-4242; www.nscfairbanks.org

About the Author

Trips around the North Country have led Montana Hodges from living in a cabin in Salcha to jumping in the Arctic Ocean at Prudhoe Bay. Through years of adventure she has traveled every inch of Alaska highway including the Marine Highway. She has written several other FalconGuides including *Camping Alaska*, a guide to 300 of the state's best road-accessible campgrounds.

WHAT'S SO SPECIAL ABOUT UNSPOILED, NATURAL PLACES?

Beauty   Solitude   Wildness   Freedom   Quiet   Adventure
Serenity   Inspiration   Wonder   Excitement
Relaxation   Challenge

There's a lot to love about our treasured public lands, and the reasons are different for each of us. Whatever your reasons are, the national **Leave No Trace** education program will help you discover special outdoor places, enjoy them, and preserve them—today and for those who follow. By practicing and passing along these simple principles, you can help protect the special places you love from being loved to death.

THE PRINCIPLES OF LEAVE NO TRACE

- Plan ahead and prepare
- Travel and camp on durable surfaces
- Dispose of waste properly
- Leave what you find
- Minimize campfire impacts
- Respect wildlife
- Be considerate of other visitors

Leave No Trace is a national nonprofit organization dedicated to teaching responsible outdoor recreation skills and ethics to everyone who enjoys spending time outdoors.

To learn more or to become a member, please visit us at www.LNT.org or call (800) 332-4100.

Leave No Trace, P.O. Box 997, Boulder, CO 80306